The Unlocking Femininity gals have masterfully intertwined the truth of scripture with the practical outworking of every day dating life. They answer the difficult questions single women are asking today with answers that speak to the heart and soul. *Radical Dating* will not only transform your dating life, but may very well make a radical difference in all areas of your life.

Terri Stovall,
Dean of Women's Programs, Associate Professor of Women's Ministry
Southwestern Baptist Theological Seminary, Fort Worth, Texas

Relationships matter to God so the way we treat each other should matter to us as well. Here is a book that takes a serious look at what it means to march to the rhythm of a different drumbeat. It will make you think and, if you're in a relationship, we hope it will make you talk.

Ian and Ruth Coffey,
Moorlands College, Sopley, Christchurch, Dorset, England

Most books on dating are so superficial as to be of no use to the thoughtful Christian. Here at last is a book that is contemporary, fun to read, and profoundly biblical. Again and again, the authors take us back to Scripture to provide a new way of thinking about dating. This book will be a lifeline to single Christians who want to date the right way, which is to say God's way.

Ray Pritchard,
President, Keep Believing Ministries, Tupelo, Mississippi
Author of *An Anchor for the Soul*, *The Healing Power of Forgiveness*,
and *The ABCs of Wisdom*

Though focused on the reader's romantic life, the consistent theme of *Radical Dating: When God Takes Over Your Love Life* poses the question, "do you *really* believe that there is *no good thing* that your heavenly Father will withhold from you *if* you are walking uprightly?" (Ps. 84:11) Sarah's, Gabrielle's, and Diane's sound biblical foundation, charming illustrations and humor pose the volume to be one that should be a part of every Christian's library.

Patricia Ennis,
Distin r of Homemaking and
omemaking Programs,
ary, Fort Worth, Texas

Are you looking for some fresh, new, solid relationship advice? Then put away those glossy women's magazines and curl up with a copy of *Radical Dating*. These girls tell it like it is. They'll challenge you to align the why, how, who, what and when of your love life with the truth of God's Word. And nowadays ... that's a truly radical thing to do!

Mary A. Kassian,
Professor, Southern Baptist Theological Seminary, Louisville, Kentucky
Author of *Girls Gone Wise*

"The Girls" (Diane, Gabrielle, and Sarah) understand the importance of centering every area of life around Christ. In *Radical Dating*, they grapple honestly, earnestly and winsomely with how young women can honor the Lord in their interactions with guys, and how bringing Him into those relationships – even into the disappointment of unfulfilled longings – can help cultivate Christ-like character.

Nancy Leigh DeMoss,
Radio host, Niles, Michigan
Author of *Revive Our Hearts*

The three authors of *Radical Dating* share some common denominators:

- deep commitment to Christ,
- theological training,
- comfort in their friendship and joy in their fellowship.

But for this project, they find strength in their common passion – preparing the next generation of women for lives set apart unto the Lord Jesus! That is a radical goal and requires radical thinking! Dating can be frivolous and futile or Christ-honoring and life-changing – all to be determined by how you go about it. This volume is a must read for young women and their parents!

Dorothy Kelley Patterson,
Professor of Theology in Women's Studies,
Southwestern Baptist Theological Seminary, Fort Worth, Texas

Radical
Dating

*When God takes over
your love life*

DIANE MONTGOMERY, GABRIELLE PICKLE AND SARAH BUBAR

CHRISTIAN
FOCUS

Copyright © Unlocking Femininity 2012
Diane Montgomery, Gabrielle Pickle and Sarah Bubar

paperback ISBN 978-1-78191-058-0
epub ISBN 978-1-78191-079-5
Mobi ISBN 978-1-78191-080-1

Published in 2012
by
Christian Focus Publications Ltd.,
Geanies House, Fearn, Ross-shire,
IV20 1TW, Scotland, United Kingdom

www.christianfocus.com

Cover design by Paul Lewis

Printed by Bell & Bain, Glasgow

CONTENTS

Section 4: What You Do on the Date – *Purity*

Section 5: When The Dates End – *Singleness*

Dedication

This book is dedicated to our readers – you girls who have chosen to live radically in the world, seeking to glorify God in all areas of your love life.

A special thanks to Dr. Dorothy Patterson, our teacher, mentor and original cheerleader! And to Alex, first for loving (and marrying) our Diane and second for being such an amazing support behind the scenes of all we've done through *Unlocking Femininity*. A huge thanks to our families, friends and churches for keeping us sane, focused and in the Word during the whole writing process. And most of all, to our Savior Jesus Christ, this book is inspired by your Word, and we pray it brings you glory.

Meet the Girls

This book began as a blog, which started as a far-fetched dream of seminary girls sitting around a table in a sushi restaurant trying to figure out how to use our years of intense Biblical training to help girls apply God's Word to everyday life. After much prayer and some research, the website UnlockingFemininity. com was born! We use this writing ministry to provide girls with a resource on topics such as gender roles, relationships and applying Scripture to everyday life.

We are best friends. We've supported each other through graduations, mission trips, first jobs, and moving away. All three of us love sushi and have made ourselves positively sick on Diane's homemade red velvet cupcakes. Even now that we have "grown up" and moved away from each other, somehow we still find time to talk, email and text....way too often.

Diane is known for "keeping it real". A natural hostess, she is famous for her Saturday morning breakfasts of syrup cups (waffles) and bacon! D is the fiercely loyal friend (aka "Mama Bear") who will always tell it like it is.... even if it means admitting you really do look fat in those jeans. An amazing athlete, she still plays competitive tennis and the girls are convinced that she could take them in a fight. She encourages young women to understand how God's loving plan sets them free to live in His hope. Diane graduated in 2011 with her Master of Divinity in Women's Studies from Southwestern Baptist Theological Seminary and now she and husband Alex serve as missionaries in South America, working with college students.

Gabrielle is known to everyone as the tall girl in even taller heels. She expresses her creativity in writing, cooking, making movies, and dyeing her hair. Gabs is a girly-girl adventurer; she hiked through the jungles of Indonesia and rode on elephants while wearing earrings and eyeliner! She is always on a new "kick', whether it is eating organic, running marathons, studying body language, or making homemade lotion. She was the first of the girls to graduate from Southwestern Baptist Theological Seminary in 2010 with Master of Divinity in Women's Studies. Currently, Gabrielle lives in Atlanta, discipling college-aged girls and producing a movie that will raise awareness about the human trafficking problem in her city.

Sarah is the social one. She's never met a stranger and continually amazes the other girls by knowing simply everyone! Sarcasm is her love language. She's a Yankee from New York and never passes up an opportunity to remind her friends of that fact. By far the most laid back of the group, she brings the "chill factor" when the rest of the girls are crazy passionate about a blog post. The most recent seminary graduate, she just finished her Master of Divinity in Women's Studies in 2012. Sarah loves teaching women of all ages to apply God's Word in everyday life, and now gets to do that full-time as the Dean of Women at Word of Life Bible Institute's Florida Campus.

Even though we are three unique individuals, we have the important things in common. Each of us has a personal relationship with Jesus Christ. We consistently encourage each other to chase after Jesus. And all of us are committed to helping women draw closer to Christ.

Introduction

Why does dating matter?

Why would anyone want or need to read yet another book about relationships?

We already know how to walk away if he's just not that into you, how to be your own matchmaker and how to make every man want you. What more does a girl need to know?!

THE TRUTH.

But more specifically, we need to know God's truth, His truth about how you date, who you date, how to spend your time while you're not on a date, and how you go about life before the wedding date.

Boys. Dating. Relationships. Singleness. We've been there. We've felt the butterflies. We've suffered through the awkward first dates. We've wondered if he would ever call. We've made the mistakes. We've struggled to recover from heartbreak. We've battled loneliness. We've questioned the point of dating and relationships.

And chances are, we've asked the same questions....

What if there is more to my love life than a never-ending pursuit of romantic bliss? What if all this boy-girl stuff has a bigger purpose than just my fleeting happiness?

What if God has a bigger plan for my dates, relationships and singleness? What if all this romantic hoop-la was not just about a boy, or several boys, but about a Savior? What if singleness, relationships and even marriage were ways for me to proclaim Christ to the world?

> Therefore, I urge you brethren, by the mercies of God, **to present your bodies a living and holy sacrifice acceptable to God, which is your spiritual act of worship.** And do not be conformed to this world, but be transformed by the renewing of your mind, so that you may prove what the will of God is, that which is good and acceptable and perfect.
>
> (Rom. 12:1-2)

What is a living sacrifice? Everything we do in life – eating, hanging with friends, serving at church, crushing on boys – is part of our sacrifice of worship to God. The question then must be asked: is our sacrifice pleasing to God? As children of God, our daily routine is about more than just eating and walking and talking and sleeping…. It's about proclaiming the name of Jesus as a witness to the world. We are to offer the area of boys, dating, relationships, and girly dreams as a living sacrifice of worship to Jesus Christ, who gave Himself up for us. Being a single girl in dating (or not dating) relationships, means honoring God in all of her relationship interactions. That is her offering of worship to God.

And if all of our relationships are about God – knowing Him, becoming like Him, and reflecting Him to the world – then the focus of our love life isn't the butterflies in our stomach, or even the really cute guy who asked us out, but it's about God. The point, the goal, the focus of your love life is God Himself.

That means that it matters **who** we date, *because our lives are a witness to the world and a sacrifice of worship to God.* It matters if we date bad boys, lost boys or jerks. It matters that the guys in our lives love Jesus more than they love us. It matters how the relationship started, continues, and even how it ends.

This means that it matters **how** we date, *because our lives are a witness to the world and a sacrifice of worship to God*. Dating is more than just finding a good Christian guy, it matters that we establish physical and emotional boundaries, that we commit to living in purity, that we encourage one another in our walk with Christ. It also matters how we break up with a guy and go on with our lives after the relationship. Everything we do in and out of relationships is part of our witness and either brings glory to God or harms His reputation.

This means that it matters **why** we date, *because my life is a witness to the world and a sacrifice of worship to God*. Dating and relationships aren't to be our identity – Christ alone defines us. As such, it matters how we handle singleness, combat loneliness, pursue relationships, and respond to guys who express their interest. The success of our relationships is founded in our understanding of God's plan and purpose for our love life.

This may seem like an extreme perspective on dating, but when God takes over your life, your love life is included. Surrender to the Lord cannot be partial if it is to be radical. We cannot pick and choose what we allow God to have a say in. That is not a living sacrifice. That is convenient Christianity.

So, ask yourself: Are you truly ready to live radically? Are you ready for God to take over your love life? He is!

SECTION 1

Why You Date:

True Love

1

How Love Died

GABRIELLE PICKLE

It was Valentine's Day weekend. I had my favorite candy in one hand and popcorn in the other, with my best girls to keep me company. It should have been the perfect drama-free night of laughter, girl-talk and a completely typical romantic comedy. Forty-five minutes later, my hopes for a happy, mindless girls night went down in flames as we watched the worst Valentine's Day love story ever. I walked out of the theater with the sinking realization that society has absolutely no idea what love really is. Movies today are all about couples cheating on their spouses, sleeping with near strangers, emotionally devastating their partners, and hooking up out of sheer loneliness. In this movie, the only apparent sweet love scene was between a gay couple.

That is not true love! We, as a society, have no idea what love is. We are told that love is so incredibly powerful that it cannot wait. We are told that if you love someone you should be having sex with them. We are told that love is so passionate that it is painful and can harm you. We are told that love is fleeting, so grab it where ever you can – even if it destroys you. We are told that you cannot guard your heart if you want to find love, you have to put yourself out there. We are told that love is found in the blood-sucking bite of a vampire's kiss. We are told that any and every expression of love is acceptable. We are told that love is a feeling and is found in the warm fuzzies, butterflies and swelling egos that a certain person makes us feel.

As a society, we sacrifice children, marriages, health, respect, and religion on the altar of this thing called "love." If we are not careful, we will follow in the footsteps of Rome, who by the fall, practiced homosexuality, bisexuality, swinging, bestiality, and pedophilia as natural expressions of "love." When did love become an excuse for people to pursue personal gratification at any cost?

This is not love.

WHY IS SOCIETY DEVOID OF TRUE LOVE? BECAUSE WE HAVE KICKED GOD OUT OF SOCIETY:

We have banished Him from our government and made laws to exclude Him from our lives. We laugh when God is mocked in sitcoms, demeaned by movie stars and dismissed as a "nice idea" in the nightly news. We have deleted God from our school curriculum and even the mention of Him is challenged in our universities. We have manipulated science to disprove His work and even deny His existence. In many places, even church is more about people than it is about God. In some congregations, God is no longer welcome. As a society, we have kicked God out.

WHAT DO GOD AND CHRISTIANITY HAVE TO DO WITH LOVE? GOD IS LOVE:

> Beloved, let us love one another, for love is from God, and whoever loves has been born of God and knows God.
>
> (1 John 4:7)

John addresses the believers of the church, explaining the reason that we are commanded to love one another. Love comes from God alone. God is the source, author, parent, and commander of love. *Anyone who loves is born of God*, so only believers can experience true love. The only way for us to love anyone else is to first be loved by God unto salvation and to love God in return. Only out of that love relationship are we able to truly love friends, spouse, family, or children. Therefore, true romantic love between a man and a woman comes from both of them being **in God.**

> Anyone who does not love does not know God, because God is love.
>
> (1 John 4:8)

Those who know God must love because God is love and the two cannot be separated. On the flipside, one who does not know God cannot know true love, for God is love. Apart from God, we have no love to give.

> In this the love of God was made manifest among us, that God sent his only Son into the world, so that we might live through him. In this is love, not that we have loved God but that he loved us and sent his Son to be the propitiation for our sins.
>
> (1 John 4:9-10)

True love is seen in how God sent his Son to die for us. It may seem that there is nothing romantic or relational about the love expressed in Christ's dying for us, but Ephesians 5:25-28 says differently. Husbands are commanded by God to love their wives, just as Christ loved the church and gave Himself up for her. This is the Greek verb *agapaō*, meaning "to love". This word does not mean "the unconditional love that only God can show," as we may have heard in Sunday School. This is an all-in, nothing-held-back kind of love, exemplified in Christ's death on the cross and commanded of believing husbands toward their wives. The Apostle John explains *agapao* in further detail in verses 14-18.

> Beloved, if God so loved us, we also ought to love one
> another. No one has ever seen God; if we love one
> another, God abides in us and his love is perfected in
> us. By this we know that we abide in him and he in us,
> because he has given us of his Spirit.
>
> (1 John 4:14-18)

The ability to love is actually proof of our salvation. The
ability to give true love comes through God's Holy Spirit
in us, which allows us to truly love – to cherish and
treasure someone, to give ourselves wholly and safely to
someone, to overcome insurmountable obstacles in the
name of love, to stick by someone through the good times
and the bad. True love only comes through the power of
God in us.

> We love because he first loved us.
>
> (1 John 4:19)

The ability to love, the skill of loving someone, comes from
God alone. While we were still unloving and unlovely, God
loved us. That love led us to salvation. That love taught us
how to love God and love each other. We cannot give or
receive love without God.

> If anyone says, "I love God," and hates his brother, he is
> a liar; for he who does not love his brother whom he has
> seen cannot love God whom he has not seen.
>
> (1 John 4:20)

A man cannot love God and hate his brother. Neither can
a man truly love his brother if he hates God. Because true
love and God are the same thing! You cannot separate the
two for they are, by definition, intertwined and inseparable!
The only way you can learn to love is from God. The only
way you can truly love someone is by God's power in you
(via salvation).

> And this commandment we have from him: whoever
> loves God must also love his brother.
>
> (1 John 4:21)

Believers are commanded to love others. Because people
who are not in Christ do not have the power to obey
God's commands, this command applies only to believers.
Even believers cannot experience true love in their own
strength, but only through the power of God. Therefore,
a society controlled by the world is a society without
love, because lost people cannot experience true love
as God intended it. Unbelievers can feel deep affection,
consuming fascination and passionate lust, but they cannot
experience true love because they have not experienced
the true God.

WITHOUT GOD, TRUE LOVE DOES NOT EXIST.
Society banished God from their lives in the name of
personal independence and community tolerance. But
what people didn't realize is that when they removed God
from their world, they destroyed their only chance at true
love as God designed it. A culture that has rejected God
has also rejected true love. It is no wonder our society has
no idea what love is because God is love, and we have
removed God from our world.

A PERSON CANNOT KNOW WHAT LOVE IS UNTIL THEY HAVE
EXPERIENCED THE GREATEST LOVE.

> Greater love has no one than this, than someone lay down
> his life for his friend.
>
> (John 15:13)

> But God shows his love for us in that while we were still
> sinners, Christ died for us.
>
> (Rom. 5:8)

If you have never experienced the Greatest Love of all, you are missing the entire point. True love comes from a true relationship with a true God. All you have to do to experience that love is surrender your life to Jesus Christ (Rom. 10:9-10); it is that simple and that difficult. But it is the only way to experience true love (John 14:6).

If you are a believer, this chapter may have rocked your concept of love, but I want to challenge you to dig into Scripture and discover God's plan for true love in your life and relationships. Every relationship must be first founded in true love for God, then for each other.

QUESTIONS THAT MAKE YOU GO "HMMM"

1. What is your concept of true love? Is it more about feelings or more about God?

2. What is your concept of God? Does that affect your view of love?

3. Based on the Scriptures in this chapter, how should your understanding of love change? Your love for God? Your love for others? Your love for a guy?

2

The Truth about Love

SARAH BUBAR

I have sewn **one** dress in my entire life. Just one. I was 15, and it was a horrible experience. It started out as a fun project. I was really excited about the blue and white polka-dotted material, and the pattern that I had spent an hour picking out. But no sooner did I start the project than everything fell apart. It started with my losing the pattern for one of the sleeves. BIG mistake… apparently, those are important. So, I ended up using the opposite sleeve's pattern and just guessing where the darts and bullets would go. The second mistake I made was realizing that those "patterns" weren't merely suggestions; you had to actually follow them precisely if you wanted it to turn out correctly. The third and perhaps the most crucial mistake was made about half-way through the endeavor: I stopped caring and just wanted the end result. Little did I know that the end result would look nothing like the picture on the cover.

There is a radical pattern for True Love defined in Scripture. It has been laid out not only in the person and character of God, as Gabrielle wrote in the previous chapter, but also in Paul's letter to the Corinthian church in the famous "Love Chapter." It is vastly different than the world's version of love, or *societal love*. It's not even cut from the same cloth. Yet I can guarantee you that the end result of 1 Corinthians 13:4-8 radiates, protects, serves and epitomizes true love.

> Love is patient and kind; love does not envy or boast; it is not arrogant or rude. It does not insist on its own way; it is not irritable or resentful; it does not rejoice at wrongdoing, but rejoices with the truth. Love bears all things, believes all things, hopes all things, endures all things. Love never fails.

This is our standard. This is the bar. Radically different than the world's love. And any "love," societal or otherwise, that does not meet this radical standard is a cheap imitation of the real thing.

LOVE IS PATIENT AND KIND.

This truth is seen throughout Scripture as implemented by our God. We see it in Psalm 103 where God forgives all our sins – ALL of them: past, present, and future. We see it in Romans 5:8 where, because of God's great love for us, He sent His Son to redeem us. The word patience means: *to exhibit internal and external control in difficult circumstances; to be calm; to suffer long.* It carries with it the idea of forgiving the sins of the person that you love, of not holding them in judgment. This is not to say, however, that you continue to stay in an abusive relationship for the sake of love, that by loving you are patiently enduring the abuse. This is what societal love would have you believe. In movies like *Twilight* (a 2010 vampire "love" story), the starring vampire, Edward Cullen, gives the appearance of being patient with Bella, the love-struck human, even though he was fighting the urge to eat her for lunch. Equally patient, Bella would make excuses at every turn for Edward's abusive and emotionally controlling behavior. Society would like to convince you that theirs is true love. This is not true love!!! Any form of abuse is not true love. *Twilight* has it completely backwards because, in the end, Edward *does* kill her – to make their love stay alive he must! Really?! How different is God's true love in comparison to this cheap imitation! Christ *died* to pay *our* debt!

LOVE DOES NOT ENVY OR BOAST.

This is a hard standard to come to. As a society that is so "me-focused," we have learned to be innately jealous of one another. It's hard to look at a brother and sister in Christ who have something good in their lives and not think, "Man, I wish I had that," instead of, "I am so happy for them." The word jealousy means *envious; desirous of another's possessions.* The interesting thing about jealousy is that in Scripture it is used in positive *and* negative ways. In Genesis 37, Joseph's envious brothers serve as a clear and gruesome picture of what jealousy can do to a family and a person's life. Equally negative, James 4:2 gives a haunting tale of murder and strife that awaits the jealous person who is grasping for what he cannot have.

But on the flipside, there are countless times where God is attributed with being a jealous God, and in 1 Corinthians 14:2, Paul is actually encouraging the church to be earnestly desirous of the spiritual gifts, using the same word found in 1 Corinthians 13:4. We must conclude then that the focal point of jealousy is the heart of the issue. If we have a friend who seems to be a great evangelist and has a heart for witnessing – be jealous of that! Strive after that! Bring that about in your life, by all means! But your friend's marital status, or great job, or newest gadget, don't be jealous of those things! That is not true love! Society markets jealousy! Don't fall victim to their ploy.

LOVE IS NOT PROUD OR RUDE.

In other words, Love does not put itself forward, is not puffed up, is not blown up, and does not behave improperly, disgracefully, or arrogantly. When I looked up the word *proud* I was astonished by the similarity between the definition of the word *proud* and the exhibition of societal love on shows like *The Bachelor*. During season 16, the phrase, "I love how *(insert girl's name)* makes me feel," gives weight to the fact that Jake Pavelka, the Texan pilot who was ABC's Bachelor, was not thinking of the girl, but only of himself. With a philosophy that directly contradicts Scripture, Jake "followed his heart" into a relationship he summed up with the word "heat." Jeremiah 17:4 says, "The heart is deceitful and desperately wicked. Who can know it?" Following something that is desperately wicked only leads to more heartbreak and further devastation. The antithesis of love, which is so prevalently shown on shows like *The Bachelor*, is based on the way someone makes me feel, me look, me think and me want. ME! ME! ME! ME! This is not true love!

LOVE DOES NOT INSIST ON ITS OWN WAY.
Coinciding with the previous verse, Paul defines true love a step farther. Not only is it not proud or putting itself forward, but true love is not even seeking its own way or serving itself. Society on the other hand, would want to convince you otherwise. They propagate a self-serving love; if the guy you're with isn't meeting your wants, dump him.

Wayne sought his own way when asking Zoe to marry him. He didn't consider what she wanted or if she was ready to take the relationship to the next level, and in the end when she broke up with him, she was labeled the jerk. Then, not eight hours later, he made out with one of his best friends, Julia (Who's the jerk now?). Even then, they had to kiss three times before they "felt any sparks." In reality, the final "spark" was probably just hormones that they had invoked by forcing themselves to connect spurred on by the loneliness each was feeling. This is not love! It may be a good story line, but it in no way mirrors true love.

Societal love insists on its own way, pushing its own agenda in the relationship. It does not place itself in the other person's shoes; it does not consider the other person's feelings. Societal love is seen in that controlling relationship, and it is extremely me-focused and self-serving. This is not true love!

LOVE IS NOT IRRITABLE OR RESENTFUL.

In Greek, these words mean: *upset, be angered, distressed.* This is speaking to those Love/Hate relationships, those passionate relationships that are swinging from either extreme of the pendulum. One moment they are fighting, and the next they are passionately kissing. Every classic love story has one of these moments. All throughout, the relationship is so volatile they have to make out just to have some reprieve from the fighting. This is not true love! This is not to say that if you ever have an argument with the person you love that you don't really love them, but the relationship shouldn't be defined as being irritable, resentful, or combative. And as commanded peacemakers, the Christian's true love should be defined by Scripture.

LOVE REJOICES IN TRUTH AND NOT WRONGDOING.

In this one movie I saw, Liz, a quirky temp struggling to make ends meet, is less than irreproachable in her morally compromising "side-job." Although meant to be a type of comedic relief in the movie, this portrayal of societal love could not be more clearly representative of our tolerant generation. Liz ends up being completely closed off to her boyfriend, Jason, while playing a part to random men. After discovering her immoral occupation, Jason has to decide if he is going to love her and be accepting of how she chooses to pay the bills or if he's going to break up with her. In the end, he uses love to excuse the lifestyle and looks the other way. This is NOT true love! And yet, in Hosea we find a parallel story of a man commanded by God to love the prostitute, Gomer. The difference we find, however, is that in Hosea's case, it is for the purpose of redeeming for a change, not excusing behavior.

He who truly loves is going to protect his object from that which is harming it. For true love rejoices in TRUTH and not wrong-doing! In 3 John 1:4, John says, "I have no greater joy than to hear that my children are walking in truth." With true love, there is a clear distinction between acceptance and approval, a distinction that societal love blurs. Societal love would have you believe that disapproving the lifestyle or behavior of a person equals rejecting who that person is. This goes contrary to the Scriptures' teaching that we are not defined by our sin. Hosea loved Gomer and accepted *her, while he rejected the lifestyle to which she subjected herself.* He would not approve of her morally repugnant behavior, because true love rejoices in TRUTH and not in wrongdoing.

LOVE BEARS ALL, BELIEVES ALL, HOPES ALL, AND ENDURES ALL. LOVE NEVER FAILS.

The word *fail* means: *to become inadequate, to be destroyed.* In the Chinese language there is no word for *fail*, ironically enough. When approaching this verse, translators have used instead "Love never stops breathing." What a beautiful depiction of the essence of true love's tenacity. This kind of love is counter-cultural. According to *Enrichment Journal*, the divorce rate in America for first marriages is 41 percent, for second marriages, it is 60 percent, and for third marriages, it is 73 percent.[1] Our culture would have

---

1   Dennis Franck. "Single Adults – A Population Group Too Large to Ignore", *Enrichment Journal* [online journal] <http://enrichmentjournal. ag.org/200003/030_too_large.cfm>, accessed 12 July 2012.

you believe that when the going gets rough, jumping ship might be your safest bet. This is not true love! Societal love allows for divorce, and every pre-nuptial agreement proves that societal love actually *plans* for the failure of marriage. True love never fails. It never becomes inadequate. It never is destroyed by the brute force winds of reality. It never stops breathing.

So, I ask you? If you were to make a dress out of the pattern of love you are using in your life, what would the end result be? Would it be skewed, misguided, and ugly much like my first attempt at sewing? Or are you using the pattern God has given not only in His character but also in His Word?

QUESTIONS THAT MAKE YOU GO "HMMM"

1. Does the end result of your love radiate, protect, serve, and epitomize God's true love?

2. In what ways do you think society has affected how you view love?

3. What is it about the way you love or see love that must change in order to reflect the biblical love of 1 Corinthians 13?

4. How would society change if each of us patterned our love after His?

3

Captivated by His Love

DIANE MONTGOMERY

Once upon a time, there was a girl. We'll call her "D." D longed to be pretty and longed to be precious in her Daddy's eyes. But, alas, she was not. Her father worked long hours, barely talked to her and never saw her as his darling little girl. D grew up fast thinking she wasn't worth his time or his love. So she started to look to others for love and affirmation. Boys seemed to like her, so she sought their affection in whatever way she could. They made her feel pretty and wanted, even if it was just for a moment. Wasn't that what she wanted?

Boys didn't offer everything that her heart desired so D began to look again in other areas. She thought "Hmm, girls who are pretty and have perfect bodies on TV and in the magazines get lots of adoration. Maybe that's where I'll find what I need?" So D began to obsess over the bodies of the models in the magazines and the actresses on TV. But no matter how much she exercised or what diet she went on, she couldn't look like them. D then took more drastic measures to achieve that "perfect" body and get everyone's praise and adoration. But it only left her hollow inside and ashamed. Her heart and body were broken. She was of no worth to anyone, let alone

God. D was wounded and didn't know what to do or who to go to…

We have all been wounded in some sort of way. We have all sought satisfaction from sources other than the Lord. We have all gone to other lovers or idols instead of our Father in heaven. And in the end, we have all been left feeling like something was missing. Why do we do this? Why do we go to places that won't give us God?

To answer that question, I think we need to first look at what God has created our hearts to desire.

For most women, their hearts desire three core things:

1. To be pursued/romanced.

2. To make a difference in someone's life.

3. To be seen as beautiful.

Women, in general, desire love and affirmation. We desire to be captivating to someone. We want a beauty that can be seen and felt, something about us that makes a difference in this world. But we can only be truly beautiful and captivating if we are captivated by God.

Sometimes, like D, we have been wounded by someone in our lives. That sin affects us and can make us doubt whether we are actually beautiful, whether we have purpose or worth. The wounds we received and the messages they bring forth form a bond with our fallen nature as women. Since the time of Eve, we, as women, have harbored mistrust in our hearts towards God. So often we think that He's holding something good from us and He's not enough for us. We are often disillusioned and fall prey to the lies of Satan, about our looks, our worth, our personalities….etc. Satan tells us that God won't be able to give us what we want. He's not even there with you but that drink is, that boy is, that purse is right there for the taking, right now. So we grasp for what's there at the moment to satisfy us, we try to control our own lives. We believe that to have the life we want, we have to go for it and do it ourselves.

So we turn to guys, women, our bodies, fashion, or the internet – whatever it may be. But none of our other "lovers' " indulgences (drinking, sex, drugs, food, shopping, porn) really satisfy. Oh, they might feel good for a little while; they might even seem to "work." But then they increase our need to indulge again and again and we find ourselves trying to fill the leftover emptiness with them. That's what sin does. It never truly works, it never gives Truth, nor does it offer the love that Jesus Christ can. We give our hearts to all sorts of other "idols" that demand our time and thoughts. We end up giving our hearts away to those things instead of giving our hearts to the Lord.

Let's bring this home: Where do you go instead of to God when the ache of your heart begins to make itself known? Are you spending too much money, bingeing, purging, shopping, drinking, or exercising? Are you drowning your hurt in movies, internet, Facebook, or even wallowing in negative emotions? **When you let your heart focus on self-doubt, condemning thoughts, or even shame, you are faithlessly indulging in another god rather than drawing close to our Savior.**

In not turning to God, we are left to wallow in a world of emptiness and loneliness. And in the core of our hearts, we still ask: Am I lovely? Do you see me? Am I valuable and precious? In not bringing our heart's questions to God, we set ourselves up for heartbreak.

THAT BRINGS UP THE QUESTION: WHERE IS GOD IN ALL THIS? HOW CAN HE LET THIS HAPPEN TO ME?
The book of Hosea gives us a great look at God, finding other lovers than God, and why He allows us to have wounds.

For she (Gomer) said, "I will go after my lovers, who give me my bread and my water, my wool and my flax, my oil and my drink." Therefore I will hedge up her way with thorns and I will build a wall against her, so that she cannot find her paths. She shall pursue her lovers but not overtake them, and she shall seek them but shall not find them...Therefore, behold, I will allure her, and bring her into the wilderness, and speak tenderly to her. And there I will give her her vineyards and make the Valley of Achor (Trouble) a door of hope.

(Hosea 2:6-7; 14-15)

God leads us to a desert place so we will seek Him and His glory, so that we will look to Him for saving. This may seem selfish on God's part, but it is because of His great love for us (Zeph. 3:17). He knows that only He can save us, love us, and redeem us so He does what He can to bring us to Him. He loves us that much ladies!

Now the woman in this passage had been committing adultery against her husband. This book is a representation of God (Hosea) and His people (Gomer). She kept leaving him and returning to other lovers, but God in His love for her kept bringing her back. He wanted to give her hope, speak tenderly to her, and woo her. Why would God woo someone unless He found them precious and priceless? That is how He feels about all women. He wants us to find rest and satisfaction in Him. He wants to betroth Himself to us in steadfast love and mercy, with an everlasting love (Hosea 2:19; Jer. 31:3). He wants to redeem us from our lives of darkness (Job 33:28; Isa. 43:1).

WE WON'T REALLY FIND TRUE CONFIDENCE AND WORTH IN OUR LIVES UNTIL WE UNDERSTAND THIS: WE ARE PASSIONATELY LOVED BY THE GOD OF THE UNIVERSE. We are precious and beautiful to the King of Kings! Nothing we have done in the past nor will do in the future can change how much He steadfastly loves us (Pss. 33:18; 36:5; Rom. 8:38-39). The Lord "in love delivered my life from the pit of destruction, and cast all our sins behind His back (Isa. 38:17). He is merciful and gracious and the steadfast love of the LORD is from everlasting to everlasting on those who fear him (Ps. 103:17).

Even though you may not have been exactly who you or God has wanted you to be in the past, don't let shame debilitate you. Don't let Satan convince you that you are unworthy, broken or beyond repair (Ps. 147:3). God is your Healer.

The more captivated we become by Him, the more we become who we were meant to be and have peace, to have a gentle and quiet spirit, a heart that trusts in God, a spirit that has been quieted by His love and filled with His peace. God radically changes everything you are and everything you do. A woman of true beauty is a woman who is not attempting to become physically beautiful or worthy or enough in man's eyes. She knows in her heart that God finds her beautiful and has deemed her worthy. In Him, she is complete. His is the only opinion she needs. His is the only opinion that is trustworthy and true.

God redeemed you, with His love, by dying on the Cross so that you can be delivered from the darkness and sin (John 3:16). Your past sins are wiped clean and completely forgotten by Christ. When you trust in Him and believe that He is Lord and Savior of this world, you become the King's Daughter and can live a life of peace and satisfaction in Christ.

So, Daughters of the King, know that our core and primary validation comes from God. And until it does, until we look to Him for our soul's satisfaction, we will not find a lasting, true love. We must keep our gaze aimed towards the face of God, even in loneliness, heartache and longing. **People will let us down and leave us but God has told us, "I will never leave you nor forsake you" (Heb. 13:5).** Seek Him, if you don't know Him. He will be all you ever need!

Oh, remember D? There is an end to her story. She was brought to a desolate place, hit rock bottom, and could only look up to her Savior. He welcomed her back into His arms, told her how much He loved her and how precious she was to Him. He redeemed her and she has never looked back. He also redeemed her father and their relationship. Now D has an earthly father who loves her and a heavenly Father who loves her even more!

QUESTIONS THAT MAKE YOU GO "HMMM"

1. Do you have a story like "D?" Take some time to write out the story of your relationship with God.

2. How has God radically changed your relationship with Him? How has God shown you He loves you?

3. What would make you feel God wouldn't love you for who you are? Do these feelings match up with what God says in the Bible?

4. What about God's character makes you know and believe that He cherishes you?

4

The Ultimate Relationship

DIANE MONTGOMERY, GABRIELLE PICKLE AND SARAH BUBAR

WHAT WOULD YOU GIVE UP FOR TRUE LOVE?
We asked via Facebook status and were immediately inundated with responses from males and females:

- "I'd give up Diet Dr. Pepper. And I am hard-core addicted."

- "I would give up a promotion, or even my dream job."

- "I gave up gluten because my wife is allergic. No more pizza, breadsticks, cake or cinnamon buns in our house. But I love her and she is worth it."

- "A big house, or even a house in general. I'd live in a shack to be with the man I loved."

- "Proximity to family. I'd move anywhere in the world for love."

As humans, we crave this paradox called love. Whether or not we've ever experienced it, we desire it. Even when it shatters our hearts, we want it back. We are desperate to be loved. Mother Teresa said, "The hunger for love is much more difficult to remove than the hunger for bread."[1] It is why romantic stories sell book after book and movie after movie, even when the basic plot is the same. We simply can't resist a powerful, sweeping depiction of love. It's the foundation for the ultimate relationship that we all crave. Throughout history, great love stories have defined cultures, captivated entire generations, and lasted long after the civilization that created it lies in ruins.

In 15th century England, it was Shakespeare's doomed young love of Romeo and Juliet. During the time of the Knights, it was the forbidden romance of Lancelot and Guinevere. For Rome, it was a love that spanned empires in Antony and Cleopatra. For the Greeks, it was the war-inciting love between Paris and Helen of Troy. For my grandmother, it was the tempestuous civil war tale of Scarlet O'Hara and Rhett Butler. For my mom, it was some movie I've never heard of called *Love Story* that was popular in the 1970s. For my older cousins, it was the tragedy of Rose and Jack on *The Titanic*. For me and my friends it was the sweet agony of Noah and Allie in *The Notebook*. According to the high school girls in my church (and some of my friends, who will remain unnamed to protect them from mockery), their picture of true love is the angst-filled relationship of Edward and Bella in *Twilight*. It isn't just a phase for teenage girls – this longing for love is found in every age group and every culture.

This love that we crave isn't weak, easy, fluffy, or cheap. We crave an all-consuming, life-altering, die-for-you kind of love. We want a love that costs us something … costs us everything. Yet is so powerful and amazing that we are happy to give up anything in this physical world to have it. We are hungry for a love so powerful that it could destroy

---

1   Mother Teresa with Devananda, Angelo and Scolozzi, Angelo. *Jesus, The Word to be Spoken: Prayers and Meditations for Every Day of the Year,* Ann Arbor, MI: Servant Publications (1998).

us, but doesn't. As one of my friends admitted, "It isn't really love unless it has the potential to destroy you." We want a love that defines us. We want an ultimate relationship.

WHY WE CRAVE LOVE

That craving for true love each of us has? That longing to be known by someone who loves us in spite of our flaws and quirks? That is our God-created craving for Himself.

Our Maker, the God of heaven and earth, designed each of His children with a God-sized hole in our souls. He created us with a longing that only He can fulfill. And all this chasing after love on earth is the futile attempt of humanity trying to find a substitute for God.

For a long time it was hard for us grasp the pull of *Twilight*. Why did women of all ages turn to putty and melt with longing for an "Edward" to come into their life. Pasty guys with red eyes and sparkles did nothing for us. But it finally makes sense. The whole *Twilight* story, it is less about his looks and charm, and more about a love that crosses human boundaries … that overcomes all odds … that defies death … a love that is so all-consuming it lasts forever. This kind of love is exactly what we, as humans, were created by God to crave. The *Twilight* story is a cheap and incomplete imitation of the love we were designed to experience with God alone. Jesus left heaven for earth …. He overcame sin for us …. He conquered death so that we could live …. and His love for us will last for eternity. God is dangerous and powerful. He has the power to destroy us and the reason to destroy us (sin), yet He doesn't. But, where *Twilight* failed is the ending. It is a love story without redemption. Because in the end, Edward corrupted Bella, took her soul, so that they could be together.

God, on the other hand, sacrificed his Son to redeem his bride. He didn't destroy us so we could experience true love. He purified us so that we could have a relationship with Him, a relationship that ultimately saves us from our own well-deserved destruction. *But God shows his love for us in that while we were still sinners, Christ died for us.* (Rom. 5:8)

No human relationship – no matter how perfect it seems – will ever completely meet that need for love. Do you ever wonder why we constantly seek love from others, yet never feel completely satisfied? It's because God designed us for an unconditional love, and we, as humans, are flawed. God tells his people,

> For your Maker is your husband, the Lord of hosts is his name; and the Holy One of Israel is your Redeemer, the God of the whole earth he is called.
>
> (Isa. 54:5)

God is our ultimate relationship.

You long for someone to love you so much that he would die for you? *Jesus did that* (John 3:16; Gal. 2:20; John 15:13). You desire a love that will never change and never give up on you? *God's love is steadfast* (Gen. 24:27; Deut. 7:9; Pss. 52:8; 36:2, 26). You need a love that can never be taken away? *Nothing can separate you from God's love* (Rom. 8:37-39). You want a love that demands your heart, soul and strength? *God asks that of you* (Deut. 6:5; 10:12). You crave a love that transforms your entire world? *God's love gives you a whole new set of guidelines* (Deut. 11:1, 13; 1 John 5:3). You desire a love that protects you? *God is your refuge* (Ps. 36:7). You long for a love that is not based on your performance or ability to give back? *God loved you when you hated him* (Rom. 5:8). You want a love that spills over into your interactions with other people? *God's love enables you to love others* (1 Thess. 4:9; 1 John 4:7-12). You need a love that drives away the fears in life? *God's love casts out fear* (1 John 4:18).

God's love is ferocious, magnificent, demanding, and consuming. It is beautiful and it is costly. It will cost you your heart. He is asking you to give up all: the lust or impure habits that control your life, the selfishness, vanity or loneliness that controls your dating choices, doing relationships like your friends do. Total surrender. And total gain.

THE ULTIMATE RELATIONSHIP

If this is your path, if you have surrendered your life to Jesus, if your sin has been paid for by the blood of Jesus Christ, then this amazing, all-consuming, soul-filling love is yours. No matter your relationship status – you have true love. So live like it! As a child of God, you have access to the most wonderful love that will ever exist but you have a part to fulfill. Obedience, commitment, and a sold-out heart to God are required to experience the joy God offers His children. We literally owe Him our lives which are supposed to be living, daily sacrifices to God. He saved your life, He expressed His love to you in a way that can and will never be done again.

If you have read this book and realized that Christ isn't Lord of your life, then we urge you to consider making Him your true love! God sent His one and only Son to earth, to live and walk through life as a human. But the purpose wasn't to hang out with His creation. See, everyone on earth has sinned against God and because of that sin we are separated from having a relationship with God and condemned to eternal separation from Him. But He loved us so much that even when we were still sinners, Christ came to save us (Rom. 5:8). Christ's purpose in coming to earth was to pay the penalty for mankind's sins and give us the opportunity to have eternal life (Rom. 6:23). That was the ultimate showcase of true love. Christ offers you the chance for the true love, through His death and resurrection, and all you have to do is confess that Jesus Christ is your Lord and repent of your sins that separate you from God (Rom. 10:9-10). Jesus Christ is the only way to experience true joy, true peace, and true love.

The purpose in writing this book was not just to help our sisters in Christ know how to better navigate through the relationship highways; the main purpose was to help our sisters in Christ know how to better glorify their heavenly Father and learn how each one is able to experience the ultimate relationship through faith in Christ. No matter how well you do at the dating game, it's all for nothing if Christ is not at the center, being glorified in your life. Always remember, Christ is the best and only love you'll ever need, everything else fades in comparison. So seek His true love first; let it radically change you, and you'll never go wrong!

QUESTIONS THAT MAKE YOU GO "HMMM"

1. Knowing how greatly God loves you, how does your perception of yourself change? What about your perception of relationships?

2. What would you say is the status of your ultimate relationship?

3. How does your relationship with Christ impact your relationships with guys (or lack thereof)?

SECTION 2

How You Date:

Relationships

5

The Guy who gets the Girl

GARBIELLE PICKLE

Would you move to a different state for the potential of finding a man, whether God was leading you there or not?

Heather did.

Sold her apartment in LA, packed up her car and moved to Denver... because the guy/girl ratio improved in her favor. It worked. The mountain men of Denver loved her. She had dates every weekend. It was a single girl's dream come true. But she still hasn't found "the one" or even one worth a second date. Even though she gave up everything in search of love, she still hasn't found it....

"The one" is no longer an ideal, it is now the sole purpose of a single person's existence. As believers, we are called to be different than the world, even in dating. Especially in dating! Whether it be online, face-to-face or long distance – how you choose to date is a personal choice, but regardless of that choice, God must come first in the love life of a believer.

In contrast to the world's methods of achieving romance, Genesis 24 records a beautiful account of a man and a woman who allowed God to orchestrate their love story. Isaac, promised son of Abraham and Sarah, needed a wife. So Abraham instructed his most trusted servant to return to their homeland and find a wife for Isaac. So, how did the servant – Isaac's representative – go about finding a wife while keeping God first?

1. HE REALIZED THAT WHO HE MARRIED WAS VITALLY IMPORTANT.

In Genesis 24: 3-4 Abraham made his servant swear *that you will not take a wife for my son from the daughters of the Canaanites, among whom I dwell, but will go to my country and to my kindred, and take a wife for my son Isaac.* Abraham knew that it was vitally important to select a God-fearing wife for his son. Whoever a man marries will either make or break him. King Solomon, the wisest man to ever live, married unwisely and it was his downfall. *For when Solomon was old his wives turned away his heart after other gods, and his heart was not wholly true to the Lord his God* (1 Kings 11:4). A godly man will be totally committed to date (and marry) only those women who love Jesus with all their hearts. A girl's fabulous good looks can be distracting for a moment, but a man of God will rise above the physical to look for a girl whose heart belongs to God. A man of God will be committed to wait for a woman of God.

2. HE REALIZED THAT THE WOMAN HAD TO BE WILLING TO SHARE HIS CALLING.

In Genesis 24:6-8 Abraham makes his servant promise to bring the girl to the Promised Land, that Isaac could not go to her – because God had called them to this place and given them this land. Abraham even said, *But if the woman is not willing to follow you, then you will be free from this oath of mine; only you must not take my son back there.* The bottom line is that a guy who has committed to following God anywhere needs to settle for nothing less than a girl who is willing to go wherever God leads. Abraham knew this and warned his servant that if the girl, or the girl's parents, wanted Isaac to come there rather than letting the girl go to him – she wasn't the one. Abraham believed God's covenant and knew that God was making them into His chosen people and had given them a Promised Land; the Chosen People needed to live in that promised land. If God has given a man something specific to do, then the woman he marries must embrace that as her own future – or she isn't the one.

3. HE PRAYED THAT HE WOULD RECOGNIZE HER BY HER CHARACTER.

The first two stipulations eliminate a lot of potential wives, so rather than waste time wading through the remaining possibilities, Abraham's servant stopped to pray, Genesis 24:12-15. Abraham's servant had no way of knowing which girl was right for Isaac, so he asked God for a sign. But instead of praying to meet the most beautiful girl in the land, or girl from the wealthiest family, he prayed for a girl with character. He went to the well where the women came daily for water and he watched their behavior. Rebekah was being obedient and serving her family by going to the well for water. Then she showed kindness, initiative and hospitality by offering a stranger a drink of water. She then went above and beyond by offering to water his camels. Let me tell you, he didn't just ride one camel – he had a whole caravan of ten or more. Camels have four stomachs, which means they can hold a LOT of water. Pulling up water from the well for all those camels must have taken hours! But in those hours, her true character was revealed. And in those hours, Abraham's servant recognized the wife God had chosen for Isaac.

4. HE RECOGNIZED THE ANSWER TO HIS PRAYER IN HER, BUT DID NOT IMMEDIATELY PROPOSE.

He stopped and prayed, being silent before God, to know if she was really the one.

> The man gazed at her in silence to learn whether the Lord had prospered his journey or not.
>
> (Gen. 24:21)

Abraham's servant saw Rebekah's beauty and pure reputation. He didn't know if she was the one until he saw those specific character qualities in her. The biggest indicator of a godly guy? He will always go back to God in prayer before he acts. Abraham's servant prayed before he looked for the girl, and then he prayed again once he found her to make certain this was God's plan. Most guys would be so impressed or smitten that they immediately would ask her out or try to marry her, assuming that because she fit their ideal mold that she was the one. Not this guy, he backed off, probably while she spent hours watering his camels, and was silent before God until he knew. He made absolutely sure that Rebekah was God's will for Isaac before he approached her.

5. ONCE GOD CONFIRMED THAT SHE WAS THE ONE, HE STOPPED AND PRAISED GOD.

Even when he knew for certain that Rebekah was the one, he didn't immediately propose. His priorities were straight – God first.

> The man bowed his head and worshiped the Lord and said, "Blessed be the Lord, the God of my master Abraham, who has not forsaken his steadfast love and his faithfulness toward my master. As for me, the Lord has led me in the way to the house of my master's kinsmen."
>
> (Gen. 24:26-28)

Now he knows he has found the woman he came for – does he propose? No, again he turns to God. When he finds God's woman for Isaac, he stops and praises God. He never once got so caught up in the girl that he forgot Who led him to the girl. What a concept! He kept God first above all else, even romance.

6. THEN HE ACTED.

When God confirmed she was the one, he went immediately to her family, not allowing them to distract him with food or rest after his long journey. He had a mission to find a wife and he acted with confidence. He proposed.

> Then food was set before him to eat. But he said, "I will not eat until I have said what I have to say."
>
> (Gen. 24:33)

As soon as He was done praising God, he acted. He was up front about his intentions – he proposed. That takes some serious guts! They offered him food and a good night's sleep before having his long talk, but no – the man refused FOOD until he had accomplished his mission. Now that, we all know, is dedication to God's plan!

7. **He won her with the testimony of God's plan.** Genesis 24:34-49 shows how Abraham's servant convinced the family and Rebekah – not by money or flowery words – but with the testimony of how God had brought her to him. And the family just couldn't say no. It was God's plan. He gave Rebekah expensive gifts, told them of his master's wealth, but what convinced them of the rightness of this union was his testimony of how God brought Rebekah to him. He recounted all that God had done, the prayers answered, and they recognized God's hand at work. The family agreed. Rebekah agreed. And a wife had been found for Isaac.

8. **The result was a fantastic story of true and abiding love.**
The whole process sounds overly-spiritual and unromantic. But it is the first mention of true love between a couple being mentioned in the Bible.

> And Isaac went out to meditate in the field toward evening. And he lifted up his eyes and saw, and behold, there were camels coming. And Rebekah lifted up her eyes, and when she saw Isaac, she dismounted from the camel and said to the servant, "Who is that man, walking in the field to meet us?" The servant said, "It is my master." So she

took her veil and covered herself. And the servant told Isaac all the things that he had done. Then Isaac brought her into the tent of Sarah his mother and took Rebekah, and she became his wife, and he loved her.

(Gen. 24:63-67)

In today's dating-crazed society this story sounds ridiculous and old-fashioned, but it worked for them. Isaac loved Rebekah, and the two carried out God's plan for His chosen people. It didn't take 85 dimensions, or a personality test, or moving to a new city – all it took was two people committed to doing it God's way. Isaac and Rebekah's story isn't a new formula to find "the one," but a testimony of how love flourishes when God is in control.

In today's calculated dating world, full of crazed singles desperately determined to find their perfect match, we often forget that God wants control of our dating life. It is easy to let the loud commercials for quick fixes to find "the one" drown out the still small voice of God as He asks us to yield our relationships to Him.

As a believer, God should be an integral part of your dating life. No matter what type of dating you choose, whether face-to-face, online or in a different city, God needs to be Lord over all of them! Give God your love life – no matter what happens it will be far better than anything you could have manipulated into existence!

QUESTIONS THAT MAKE YOU GO "HMMM"

1. Have you given your love life to God? What areas of your dating life are you holding onto? Can you find any Scriptures that will help you give control over to God?

2. What do you want in "the one"? Does your list line up with God's list for you? (Someone who loves God first, seeks to follow God and listens to God?)

6

The Girl who gets "Got"

GABRIELLE PICKLE

"I am ready to have grandkids." My mom announced to the family a week ago.

Not exactly what any single girl wants to hear. I am the oldest of six – four girls and two boys. As the oldest, the family often looks to me as the one with the most potential to get married and produce grandkids. A fact that people never cease to remind me of. "It's not like we have a choice," my sister defended us. "Doing it God's way means we have to wait around for the guys to step up. We have NO control over the marriage and kids thing." "Yeah, talk to the boys." Another sister chimed in, "At least they can do something about it!"

Every single girl who is trying to do things God's way can relate to my sisters' frustration. God created men as the pursuers and women as the responders. It is part of the basic nature of God-ordained masculinity and femininity. Ephesians 5 presents marriage as a picture of the gospel; men are compared to Christ and women are compared to the church, His bride. Christ pursued His church; the church did not pursue Christ. Following the examples given over and over in Scripture, men are to pursue women. Period. This is seen in the biblical stories of Ruth and Boaz (Ruth 4), Solomon and his Bride (Song of Solomon), and

Isaac and Rebekah (Genesis 24) … to name a few. Even the world has realized that men are designed to pursue. The book *He's Just Not That Into You*, is based entirely on the premise that if a guy is interested, he WILL pursue the girl. Patti Stanger, the infamous Millionaire Matchmaker, teaches girls how to let the man be "the hunter male" and has a firm rule against girls calling boys in her club. "Give him space to chase!" she tells girls.[1]

So, men get to pursue…what is a girl to do?

The Bible provides a beautiful story that gives us an example of a godly woman responding in a romantic relationship. Genesis 24 not only shows us how a godly man should depend on God in his love life, but also how a godly woman responds to romantic situations in a way that glorifies God and not herself or some boy.

1. SHE WASN'T LOOKING FOR A HUSBAND.

> Before [the servant] had finished speaking, behold, Rebekah … came out with her water jar on her shoulder. The young woman was very attractive in appearance, a maiden whom no man had known. She went down to the spring and filled her jar and came up.
>
> (Gen. 24:15-16)

Drawing water was work for women and servants. Men of marriageable age were out in the fields or working with animals. Rebekah was not looking for a man at the well. She was not doing her chores to impress a boy. She was simply being responsible – doing her chores – because that was what God had given her to do. She was being the woman who God created her to be, and that alone got her noticed.

---

1   Greg Benrendt and, Liz Tuccillo. *He's Just Not That Into You*, New York, NY: Simon Spotlight Entertainment of Simon & Schuster, Inc. (2006).

2. **HER GOOD REPUTATION WAS REFLECTED IN HER DRESS AND APPEARANCE.**

> The young woman was very attractive in appearance, a maiden whom no man had known.
>
> (Gen. 24:16)

Rebekah was attractive in appearance. She didn't just throw her hair into a knot, unshowered, and wear yesterday's sweats while running around getting things done. She cared about how she presented herself as a woman of God and Abraham's servant noticed that about her. Also, she dressed in such a way as to tell the whole world that she was pure and a woman of God. The only way a stranger could tell her good reputation from one look was how she dressed. Her appropriately modest appearance conveyed her godly reputation. Are you dressing to be the center of attention or the answer to a godly man's prayer?

3. **SHE HAD NOTICEABLE CHARACTER.**

> She went down to the spring and filled her jar and came up. Then the servant ran to meet her and said, "Please give me a little water to drink from your jar." She said, "Drink, my lord." And she quickly let down her jar upon her hand and gave him a drink. When she had finished giving him a drink, she said, "I will draw water for your camels also, until they have finished drinking." So she quickly emptied her jar into the trough and ran again to the well to draw water, and she drew for all his camels. The man gazed at her in silence to learn whether the Lord had prospered his journey or not.
>
> (Gen. 24:16-21)

Rebekah extended kindness to a needy stranger. And it wasn't just a passing kindness as she returned to her chores. She saw needs and met them, even though it was time-consuming and exhausting. Not only was the servant thirsty, all the camels in his caravan were thirsty. She drew water for an untold amount of thirsty camels (a camel drinks between 30-50 gallons at a time). And she had no idea this servant was the representative of her wealthy relative, Abraham! She was beautiful, had a good reputation, was from a respected family, and yet her character out-shone all of those qualities. She didn't just bring out her character to wear as a cute accessory when the men of God came to town looking for a wife. No, it was visible to a total stranger even when she was doing chores. Her character confirmed that she was the one for Isaac.

4. SHE PRAYED AND GOT COUNSEL BEFORE SAYING "YES".

> When the camels had finished drinking, the man took a gold ring weighing a half shekel, and two bracelets for her arms weighing ten gold shekels, and said, "Please tell me whose daughter you are. Is there room in your father's house for us to spend the night?" She said to him, "I am the daughter of Bethuel the son of Milcah, whom she bore to Nahor." She added, "We have plenty of both straw and fodder, and room to spend the night." The man bowed his head and worshiped the Lord and said, "Blessed be the Lord, the God of my master Abraham, who has not forsaken his steadfast love and his faithfulness toward my master. As for me, the Lord has led me in the way to the house of my master's kinsmen." Then the young woman ran and told her mother's household about these things.
>
> (Gen. 24:22-28)

In that time, strangers did not give gifts to girls. So this gift was special. When Abraham's servant gave her the nose ring and bracelets, he was offering her the tokens of her bride price. In ancient culture, the family of the groom paid the family of the bride for the right to marry their daughter. The jewelry given Rebekah was the first part of that, followed by more jewelry, clothes, and precious things to her family (v. 53). She knew that some very wealthy man, who knew the God of her fathers, was interested in marrying her. So she did what any girl in her right mind would do … she ran home and told everyone! But she didn't say "yes". She was quite obviously excited about the possibility – what girl wouldn't be? But she gave no answer or promise. She waited until she was with her family, people whom she trusted, before she gave an answer. And it wasn't until after she heard his testimony of how God orchestrated this whole meeting that she was ready to give herself in marriage. This also was a reflection of her character; she valued her parents' advice and wasn't won over by gifts, but by the testimony of God's guidance.

Guys, can I just give one word of advice? Don't propose with a nose ring. As my Aunt Emily would say, "Tacky with a capital T!"

5. SHE TRUSTED GOD WITH THE UNKNOWN.

> But he said to them, "Do not delay me, since the Lord has prospered my way. Send me away that I may go to my master." They said, "Let us call the young woman and ask her." And they called Rebekah and said to her, "Will you go with this man?" She said, "I will go."
>
> (Gen. 24:56-61)

Her response was sure and she backed it up with action. The man pursued and she responded as soon as she knew it was God's will. That revealed a solid trust in God. She did not allow hesitation or doubt to distract her from God's plan. What courage it took for her to follow God …. and a servant she had just met … into the unknown. She was gaining a husband and a future, but losing a family and a past. It would have been very tempting for her to second guess God, but when she saw God's hand in the testimony of His servant she simply acted. She had trusted God with her future as a single woman, now she was continuing that trust as a married woman.

6. SHE WAS REWARDED WITH THE TRUE LOVE OF A GODLY MAN.

> Now Isaac had returned from Beer-lahai-roi and was dwelling in the Negeb. And Isaac went out to meditate in the field toward evening. And he lifted up his eyes and saw, and behold, there were camels coming. And Rebekah lifted up her eyes, and when she saw Isaac, she dismounted from the camel and said to the servant, "Who is that man, walking in the field to meet us?" The servant said, "It is my master." So she took her veil and covered herself. And the servant told Isaac all the things that he had done. Then Isaac brought her into the tent of Sarah his mother and took Rebekah, and she became his wife, and he **loved** her.
>
> (Gen. 24:62-67a)

It says that Isaac loved Rebekah … collective sigh. This is the first mention of a man loving his wife in the Bible. We know that Adam loved Eve and Abraham loved Sarah because of specific actions and lifestyle choices, but this is the first time the husband/wife relationship is described with the word love. That is what trusting God got Rebekah – a love story.

Rebekah didn't do anything extra special or amazing to be noticed. She was simply living the life God had given her. She was godly, responsible and trusted God with her future. And in being the woman God called her to be, she became the answer to Isaac's prayer and the love of his life.

So often, we are given a picture of the type A, get-up-and-go girl who can make her life happen. She gets the degree, job, and guy … if she wants him. Once she locates appropriate husband material, it is just a matter of time until she snags him. Psalm 139 reminds us that all of our days were written in His book before one of them came to be. If a chapter of His book for you includes marriage, then He has already written the day you will meet the one. So, put the pen down, stop trying to guess (or orchestrate) the next chapter and allow God – who loves you – control of your love story.

Will you trust God with your love life?

QUESTIONS THAT MAKE YOU GO "HMMM"

1. If you let God write your love story, how would you like for it to end? Is your heart ready to let Him write however He wants?

2. Do you trust Him that He'll write a beautiful love story for you, whether you get to fall in love with a Jacob, just God, or both?

7

"Do's" and "Don'ts" of Dating:
How NOT to be "That Girl"

SARAH BUBAR

Maybe you know "that girl," maybe she's one of your best friends, or she tried dating your brother. You nervously watched as she got her 15 minutes of fame on *that infamous dating reality show,* and she definitely has been the key influencer on a number of your own bad choices in previous budding romances. Do you know who I am talking about? She's the girl who gets a crush on a guy and immediately becomes obsessed with everything about him: his interests, his sports teams, his classes, his family. She's the reason terms like "Facebook stalking" and "Stage 5 clinger" exist. And while none of us want to be *that girl,* many times we unintentionally fall prey to her antics.

The world of dating can seem like a crazy and intimi*dating* (no pun intended!) playing field. With all the advice books laying out strategies on how to hook the man, to entire website databases engineered to find the most compatible match for you, to media-driven television shows and movies focusing on the subject, it's a wonder any of us successfully navigate through the maze known as the dating world.

As Christian women, we also find ourselves coming onto the dating scene with a quandary. How does a godly girl date, should she date, or should she just kiss the idea of dating goodbye? With so many voices in our head, it's confusing to know to whom we should listen. In this chapter, we explore some of the do's and don'ts of radical dating and how to not be *that girl* none of us want to become.

DO: *KEEP YOUR HEAD IN THE FACTS, NOT IN THE CLOUDS.*

As women, we can very quickly fall into the role of girlfriend, even if we don't possess the title to match it. It's almost a natural inclination. As women, we're highly relational, more so than guys because we were created to be relational people, first relating to God and then to others. We love connecting with others, learning about their lives, and deepening friendships. For women, when we relate, we bond. But bring this bond-forming characteristic into a relationship with a guy, and it can stifle a relationship before it even has an opportunity to develop. Guys consider this clingy. They imagine you've taken on the persona of a "crazy-stalker lady" who has the two of you married with 3.5 children when you haven't even had one date yet.

This may seem extreme and sound like "crazy-talk," but how many of us can semi-relate to these impulses? We like a guy, find him intriguing, and therefore, we want to find out everything we can about him. But in order to not become *that girl* we must keep our heads in the facts, not in the clouds. The facts are: if he's talking to you, it might mean he's just friendly, and not necessarily interested in you. If he winks at you, it probably doesn't mean, "Come hither." It could just be a habit he has. Winking doesn't always mean what we want it to mean. I have this one guy friend who winks when he's joking around with you. I know he's not interested, partly because he's like a younger brother and also because he was interested in a friend of mine, and when he talks, at times, he winks. I don't think anything of it. I had to remember this fact when this other guy I was interested in winked at me.

The fact is: If a guy is interested in you, he'll let you know ... trust me. When a guy is genuinely interested in developing a relationship with a girl, he'll do more than just simply have conversations with her; he will be intentional in getting to know her. He will ask her out on dates and communicate how he feels about her. He will be the one to pursue all contact. This is important to remember when the temptation comes to open lines of communication. Most guys are not going to be mean, so if you text or call them first and you're friends, they are going to respond. This should not be confused with interest on their part. You have put them in a situation where they have to choose between being rude and being nice; most guys are going to choose being nice. But if you resist being the first to text, call or talk to him, and he does come and talk to you, then you know that it's because he's genuinely interested and not just being nice.

DON'T: *HAVE TUNNEL VISION.*

As girls, we can become engrossed over anything: fashion trends, celebrity news, novel series. Anything can become our next fixation, including a crush. The biggest problem with obsession is the all-consuming tunnel-vision we acquire. We become so focused on our obsession that everything else fades into the background. When it comes to *that* guy, there are certain things we can do to make sure we don't suffer from tunnel-vision.

First, *DON'T be aware of his every move.* This is sometimes hard for us. I was talking to my friend about this guy I was interested in once A large group of us were sitting outside between a class break and this guy happened to join us after awhile, standing next to me. I told my friend how one moment he was there and the next moment he was seven feet away walking back to class. She was surprised that I hadn't even noticed he had left the group. For much of my dating life and for most of us women, it's instinctual to be aware when the guy you're interested in walks into a room. It's not like you're surveying the sea of faces to find him. You just naturally know where he is, who he's talking to. But if you don't want to become preoccupied with him, you need to resist the urge to track him around the room.

Second, *DON'T text him all the time.* This "don't" is particularly hard for those of us who are highly communicative. We (and I say "we" because I sometimes have to put the phone down and walk away because the temptation is so strong) want to know what they're doing, how a certain event went, or what they had for lunch and if it was any better than the soup we had. It can be very easy to justify a quick little text. I remember one very humbling moment for me that occurred not too long ago. I was into this guy and he hadn't texted me for like 18 hours! I was dying. I had no good reason to text him, no information to relay or question to ask. I simply just wanted to talk to him, even if it was about nothing consequential. I actually contemplated "accidentally" sending him a question I was going to send my girlfriend, just so he could text back and I could be like, "Oh, sorry. That was meant for someone else. Anyways, how are you?" And the desired conversation would ensue. I was humbled in that moment when the true nature of my manipulative heart was revealed. I put the phone down and said to myself, "No, Sarah. You are *not* going to manipulate this. If he was wondering how you were doing, he would've texted you. If he's not then, he's just not that into you. Either way, it's not your concern. Step away from the phone."

We all have these moments of battling what we want to do with what we should do. If we want to find the way through the dating arena in a biblical manner, we must resign to the fact that what we **should do** should always win out in the end. But this is tough at times ... I get it! It takes a certain level of determination to say "no" to every whim of the heart. But the more good choices we make in this adventure, the easier it will become to make those same wise choices again.

Lastly, *DON'T spend every day with him*. Resisting this urge will help balance out the natural inclinations of obsession. If you're finding yourself overly infatuated with a guy, chances are you're spending way too much time (alone or otherwise) with him. Begin limiting your time together. This doesn't mean you never hang out with him or talk with him; but a balance should occur which matches the level of your commitment to each other. If you're acting like a girlfriend without actually being his girlfriend and you do ever become that to him, you will have nowhere to grow in your relationship because you've already been there fulfilling that role.

DO: *Use caution when telling about your life.*

Sometimes as women, we can talk too much. I know, this accusation sounds bizarre and unfounded, but it's true. We are talkers. For those of us with the "gift of the gab," we tend to over-share information about our lives to people who have not yet earned the right to that information by way of a committed relationship. It's a tricky balance to know what to share and what not to share with a guy who seemingly is expressing interest. On one hand, you want him to have the information he is seeking, learn more about you, and have stimulating conversations with him. But on the other hand, sharing too much information creates a false sense of intimacy that can confuse the reality of the situation. A good rule of thumb in avoiding this behavior is to pray right before you're about to reveal that deep, dark secret that only one other person in the world knows. Ask the Lord if He thinks it's the right time to share that story or to reveal that information. As a relationship develops, you will need to balance limiting information with controlled disclosure if you want your relationship to continue to grow to the next level. But at the beginning, use caution when sharing about your life and emotional baggage. Too much too soon is what *that girl* does.

DO: *HAVE QUALITY TIME WITH YOUR GIRL FRIENDS.*
It's not absurd to spend a good amount of time together when you're first starting to talk to a guy. This is how you get to know each other. He asks you out on dates, you sit and talk about your lives, commonalities, and interesting differences. All of it can be extremely fascinating, not to mention fun. But when you're not yet in a committed relationship with a guy, balance is the key for maintaining a healthy relationship. When you're just hanging out with friends, don't use that time to talk about your guy. Use it to fellowship with your girl friends, cultivating those relationships as well. They're important friendships needed to bring balance and accountability into your life.

DO: *BE OPEN AND HONEST WITH YOUR ACCOUNTABILITY.*
This is probably one of the most important "do's" on this list because accountability is paramount to not becoming *that girl* whom you don't want to become. Your accountability will help you see areas where you're doing well and areas that need improvement. Friends can look at the budding romance objectively, without any emotions involved and help you decipher the facts from speculations. They're your voice of reason when feelings are running amuck, and they're invaluable to your success. Don't go without them!

So there you have it: the do's and don'ts of the dating world. While this list is not meant to be exhaustive, it does give you some practical ideas and challenges you can start practicing now in your life. The bottom line is if we are actively seeking to trust God with our love life, or lack of one, we'll never become *that girl* because she's a woman who trusts in her own abilities to get the guy, not in God's capability to orchestrate her life. She is looking at the small picture, the void in her life which can seem expansive, massive and all-consuming. Her loneliness focuses her in on herself and what she is living without. But the girl who is radically trusting God knows that He's got this. Psalm 84:11 is her motto, "For the LORD God is a sun and shield; the LORD bestows favor and honor. No good thing does he withhold from those who walk uprightly." The woman who is radically trusting God is focused on bringing Him glory in every season of her life, and as she realizes her contentment is found in her relationship with God, she knows she's never really alone.

QUESTIONS THAT MAKE YOU GO "HMMM"

1. When you think a guy might be interested in you, how can you stay focused on the facts of the situation?

2. What are some ways that you KNOW guys show a girl he's interested in her?

3. Instead of becoming completely focused on your new crush, what are some ways you can focus on other things instead?

4. How can you bring God glory when you're crushing?

8

How to be a godly Girlfriend

DIANE MONTGOMERY

When I stopped being someone's girlfriend and became someone's wife, it was a bit strange to adjust to the thought that never again would I be a girlfriend. Were all those years reading books and magazine articles on being the "perfect" girlfriend all for nothing? Absolutely not! Those years taught me so many lessons and also laid the foundation for my marriage and who I am as a wife today. God used those times of being a girlfriend to change how I viewed being a wife, how I viewed love, how I viewed godliness. And, believe me, God's viewpoint of what it takes to be a girlfriend was radically different than what I read in all those books and magazines. God's lessons were based on Scripture, which is the most counter-cultural thing known to man.

To be the best, most godly girlfriend possible, you've got to base your qualities on some radical ideas: the Bible. But what does this girlfriend look like? What must be so radically different about her compared to the "Be a Great Girlfriend in 10 Easy Steps" article in the latest fashion magazine?

1. CHRIST IS HER FIRST LOVE.
First off, she's must be godly of course. This may seem very basic but this is the most foundational and most radical

trait for being a good girlfriend. Any girl that does not have Christ as her center, her all, her everything, will not be able to become the godly girlfriend or have the most healthy and God-honoring relationship. She will be in danger of having her boyfriend become her center, her all, her everything, which is honestly, idolatry. Anything that comes first in your heart, before Christ, is that very thing that we're commanded against.

> Now, what does the LORD your God require from you, but to fear the LORD your God, to walk in all His ways and love Him, and to serve the LORD your God with all your heart and with all your soul.
>
> (Deut. 10:12)

> Beware that your hearts are not deceived, and that you do not turn away and serve other gods and worship them.
>
> (Deut. 11:16)

Over, and over and over again, the Bible commands for God's followers to love Him with ALL their hearts and ALL their souls. This is the greatest command of all. (Mark 12:28-30) We must love God foremost before we can ever hope to love a boyfriend or husband in a godly and Christ-like way.

2. HER CONFIDENCE AND ASSURANCE COMES FROM CHRIST. She knows who she is in Christ and exactly how He feels about her. She doesn't need to fish for compliments or need constant assurance of how her boyfriend feels about her. I tended to worry a lot when I would be in relationships. In my insecurity, I would worry about the future of my relationship with the guy, how he felt about me, or if he found me attractive enough. In my insecurity, I grasped for confidence from him, grasped for anything that would give me assurance that I was cared for by him. Every time

I grasped for a guy's assurance I would be let down and left wanting. I was like the ones spoken about in John 12:43: **For they loved the approval of men rather than the approval of God.** I was not trusting or seeking the Lord for love and security; I was seeking and trusting in sinful, flawed men.

A godly girlfriend, however, is like the woman in Proverbs 31:25: **Strength and dignity are her clothing, And she smiles at the future.** She walks with her head high and a smile on her face because she knows she's the daughter of the one and only eternal King. She fears the Lord, and trusts in Him and in His promises for her. She looks to Him for her strength, for her confidence and she is never left wanting. He fulfills and satisfies her completely because she has been changed by His saving grace! This radically changes in whom and in what you put your confidence.

> And we know that God causes all things to work together for good to those who love God, to those who are called according to [His] purpose.
>
> (Rom. 8:28)

Don't get me wrong; hearing your boyfriend's compliments about you or hearing how he feels about you is great to hear, and he should definitely be showing you that he cares for you, but be careful if that brings a smile to your heart more than knowing that the God who created you loves you more and thinks you are far more beautiful than any earthly man could.

3. She Encourages Him Spiritually and Emotionally

Since the godly girlfriend's center is Christ, she is able to encourage her boyfriend with her faith and encourage him in his walk as well. This can be as simple as saying to each other, "Ok, God is way more important to me than you and I need my time with Him, so tonight we're going to end hanging out earlier than usual" or "What did you learn at church today?"

Your relationship should be like a triangle: Christ at the top, you and he are on the bottom, building each other up towards becoming closer to Christ.

> Therefore encourage one another and build each other up…
>
> (1 Thess. 5:11)

> That is, that we may be mutually encouraged by each other's faith.
>
> (Rom. 1:12)

While the godly girlfriend encourages her boyfriend's personal walk with God, she does not lead him in it or to it. For example, he should already be actively going to church, not going just because she started taking him. She is an encourager, not an enforcer or leader. The man's role is to be the leader, and he must have his own separate walk for which he is responsible for making strong. You must both have independent, growing relationships with Christ, and you must both be sharpening and encouraging each other in those walks.

Godly girlfriends build their boyfriends up spiritually, and they also build them up emotionally. Guys need respect and need to know they are respected. They need their girlfriends to verbalize that they're proud of them. If your boyfriend got a scholarship, got a job promotion or hit a home-run at his game, then let him know how proud of him you are. Always encourage him in whatever he is doing well.

> The wise woman builds her house…
>
> (Prov. 14:1)

> It is better to dwell in a corner of the housetop [on the flat oriental roof, exposed to all kinds of weather]

than in a house shared with a nagging, quarrelsome, and faultfinding woman.

(Prov. 21:7)

4. SHE IS INTERESTED IN HIS INTERESTS

Let each of you look not only to his own interests, but also to the interests of others.

(Phil. 2:4)

A good and godly girlfriend, not only supports her boyfriend spiritually and emotionally, but she also supports him and his hobbies. Before my husband dated me, none of his girlfriends had supported the many sports he played and he LOVES sports. They are a big part of his life so I knew that if I went to support him when he was playing softball or volleyball, it would mean the world to him. I didn't always feel like going but because I cared about him, I went and actively supported his interests.

Your boyfriend may not be interested in sports but does he love books, video games, etc? Play a video game with him sometimes. Go to a bookstore together sometime. Believe me, he will love it. It shows that you care about HIM and things that matter to him, not just what matters to you.

5. SHE DOES GOOD THINGS FOR HIM AND HE TRUSTS HER

The heart of her husband trusts in her, and he will have no lack of gain. She does him good, and not harm, all the days of her life.

(Prov. 31:11-12)

Before the godly girlfriend becomes a godly wife she must be open, honest, and trustworthy. Her lifestyle must show her godliness. Her boyfriend will trust her based on how she lives out her life. If she tells him how she went and told a bunch of people a very private secret her friend shared with her, he will automatically know he can't trust her with anything he would want to share with her.

As a wife, there are things, such as making my husband dinner or folding his laundry, that didn't just start when I got married. There wasn't a "do good things for him" switch that automatically turned on once I said "I do." That goes against my very nature as a sinful human so I had to start practicing way before I even met Alex.

When we were dating, if I went to Wal-Mart to get some things, if I knew he needed something, I would go ahead and get it for him. I tried to actively think about him and what I could do for him. You don't have to be a good cook, baker, or skillful at anything to do good to your boyfriend. You just have to be thoughtful.

6. SHE HAS A LIFE.

Not only does the godly girlfriend have her own spiritual life but she also HAS A LIFE, a life outside of her boyfriend. When she is in a relationship, she doesn't forget the ones who love her most and have her best interests in mind. Instead, she keeps them close and makes time for them.

> Where there is no guidance the people fall, But in abundance of counselors there is victory.
>
> (Prov. 11:14)

> Two are better than one because they have a good return for their labor. For if either of them falls, the one will lift up his companion. But woe to the one who falls when there is not another to lift him up.
>
> (Eccles. 4:9-10)

In the Song of Songs, the Old Testament book about two people who were madly in love with each other, the friends were actively involved in the relationship between the man and the woman. Even though this is their love story, the friends are still seen protecting, encouraging, and holding accountable their beloved friend. For your own benefit and for the benefit of your relationship, keep your friends close. You'll never regret building your friendships, but you will regret neglecting them.

She also doesn't throw away her own interests and desires just because she has his to be involved with. Even though I became involved in Alex's sports, I kept my interests. I went to his games and he went to my tennis tournaments. I still kept up those things that I loved and what made me who I am in part. Don't forget that your interests and hobbies make you unique and special.

Godly girlfriends still go after the plans the Lord has for them. They keep seeking His will for their lives, not His will for their relationships. Up until Alex and I were engaged, I did not make my future plans the same as his. I did not know if we were going to get married so I kept on with the plans I knew the Lord had for me at that point. I didn't go and change my degree to match his or start to plan on living where he was. I didn't plan my life around him but I planned it around what I knew for sure God had for me at that moment in my life.

> Trust in the LORD with all your heart and do not lean on your own understanding. In all your ways acknowledge Him, And He will make your paths straight.
>
> (Prov. 3:5-6)

What this all boils down to is: Is Christ your first love? Do you date godly guys? Are you thoughtful of the other person when you're in a relationship? When these three things are in check and God is at the center of your dating life then the dating road will be a lot less bumpy. Of course, not every relationship will end in marriage but each one will be healthier, more God-honoring, and filled with a lot less regret because God was in control on both ends. You'll be a godlier girlfriend with a dating life more reflective of Christ.

QUESTIONS THAT MAKE YOU GO "HMMM"

1. How do you, as a girlfriend, reflect Christ right now?

2. What are some small steps you can take towards being a good, godly girlfriend?

3. What is something thoughtful you can do for your boyfriend tomorrow?

4. How can you help your boyfriend grow closer to the Lord?

5. How does being a good girlfriend draw you closer to God? How can you give Him glory through being a girlfriend?

SECTION 3

Who You Date:

Boys

9

Can Bad Boys be godly Men?

Diane Montgomery

As I approached leaving the dating life forever to get married to the godliest man I had ever known, it made me look back at the dating process and all the different types of men I had met and sometimes, unfortunately, dated. There's the intellectual type, the athletic guy, the funny man, and then there are the bad boys. Oh, the bad boys. These guys are different. The secular world has them, and the Christian dating sphere isn't without its share as well. They're smooth, confident, mysterious and used to give me a flurry of butterflies. They were just a step above the rest of normal guys…or so I thought. They were saved, so that ensured a God-honoring dating relationship, right? Unfortunately, I learned the hard way that the answer is NO.

Many women have the same pull towards bad boys. What is it about them that attracts so many ladies, even Christian women? They know exactly what to say to each woman to make her feel special. They're confident, knowing what they want and don't mind putting their egos at stake to ask you out. They have a rebellious side, live with a "devil-may-care" attitude and are fiercely independent. All these different things make up a guy that is exciting to us: he's usually popular, attractive, and fulfills some need of acceptance and significance. Add being a Christian to these characteristics, and it seems like you have the perfect man. But just because he may have his "fire insurance" (salvation), as one of my friends puts it, does that make him the kind of man you should date or eventually marry? Does his character match up with how the Bible defines a godly man? Is he radically changed by Christ and worthy of dating a radically changed daughter of God?

WHY BAD BOYS CAN'T BE GODLY MEN

1. THEY PUT THEMSELVES FIRST ABOVE ALL OTHERS AND ONLY WANT YOU FOR WHAT YOU CAN DO FOR THEM.
These kinds of Christian men cannot offer you the sacrificial love that God commands of husbands in Ephesians 5:25-30. A bad boy shows you attention, gives you constant compliments and excitement, but when you stop meeting his needs and making him happy, he will lose interest in you. He will get bored and move on to the next woman or thing that fulfills his selfish desires. God commands in Philippians 2:3-4:

> Do nothing from rivalry or conceit, but in humility count others more significant than yourselves. Let each of you look not only to his own interests, but also to the interests of others.

Christian bad boys can't be godly men until they become humble and self-sacrificial, which are the signs of a biblical and godly man who has been radically changed by Christ's transforming salvation. Unless the bad boy learns true humility, he has no chance of being the sacrificial husband and father God commands him to be (Eph. 5:25-30).

2. THEY'RE SMOOTH TALKERS.
Bad boys tell you exactly what you want to hear, what makes you feel good about yourself. But what they say is

usually not at the appropriate time (premature commitment talk), and it is usually not genuine. Most of the time selfish motives are behind every word. The Bible calls this flattery (Pss. 5:9; 12:2; 78:36; Prov. 29:5). In Romans 16:17-18, Paul writes about false prophets who shared this very same characteristic:

> I appeal to you, brothers, to watch out for those who cause divisions and create obstacles contrary to the doctrine that you have been taught; avoid them. For such persons do not serve our Lord Christ, but their own appetites, and by smooth talk and flattery they deceive the hearts of the naive.

Christian bad boys can't be godly men until they speak truth with their mouths and do not use flattery to serve their selfish desires. Smooth but empty words, charming but untrustworthy personalities only cause division, insecurity, and isolation from the best things in your life.

3. THEY ISOLATE WOMEN FROM GODLY FRIENDS AND FAMILY.
Many times the bad boy tries to keep you away from your friends and family in very sly ways. As one friend shared, her boyfriend used to say "Oh, let's have dinner just you and me this time and not go over to your family's house," or "Let's not sit with your family in church, your mother's singing annoys me." Does your bad boy try to spend as little time as possible with your family? What does your family think of him? If your parents are godly, you should heed their advice. Too many times I thought I knew better than my parents when it came to my dating relationships. Finally, I realized my parents had wisdom and saw things that I couldn't about the guys. It would have saved me so much heartache, helped me honor my parents, and build a stronger relationship with them if I had listened to them more often.

Christian bad boys also isolate you from godly friends. They try to make sure all time together is spent alone and even try to discourage you from maintaining your friendships. They do this because they know those who love you have your best interests in mind and the bad boy is not in your best interest. Proverbs 18:1 is a great biblical example:

> Whoever isolates himself seeks his own desire; he breaks out against all sound judgment.

The Christian bad boy isolates himself from sound judgment and will try to get you to join him. Until he seeks godly advice and wants to surround himself (and you) with godly people, he cannot be a godly man. A girl once shared with me about her relationship with a Christian bad boy, "It felt like it was him and me against the world, but then I realized that the world was everyone who would lay down their lives for me." He had isolated her from all her friends. After having ended a relationship, have you had to mend friendships or family relationships because of neglect or disregard of their sound advice? You just might have been dating a bad boy.

4. They don't protect your heart or your body.
They have no boundaries, physically or emotionally. Protecting your heart goes back to their smooth-talking tendencies. All those compliments he gave you may have been nice to hear but was it nice for your heart? Was it said at an appropriate time? 1 Corinthians 10:23-24 says:

> "All things are lawful," but not all things are helpful. "All things are lawful," but not all things build up. Let no one seek his own good, but the good of his neighbor.

While I was dating my husband, Alex, he didn't just blurt out what he felt about me early on in the relationship, but only what was for my good. He could have told me exactly what I wanted to hear and flattered my ears, but instead he was patient, kind, and not self-seeking. Alex waited for the appropriate time to share his feelings about me and our future – once he knew it was for my good and, also, God-honoring. For our relationship, this meant even not saying "I love you" until Alex knew he could follow it with a lifelong commitment and proposal of marriage. Was that hard not to hear those three words every girl wants to hear for nine long months? Absolutely! But I know Alex was doing it to protect me and our relationship and make sure we were honoring God. In order for your heart to be protected, there must be separation from any romantic feelings and following 1 Corinthians 13. Is your bad boy protecting your heart and not awakening love until it so desires (Song 2:7)?

Is your bad boy protecting your heart and your body? 1 Corinthians 6:18 says to "Flee from sexual immorality." Fleeing from sin means there have to be boundaries before the physical element enters the relationship. Does he compromise those physical boundaries by "accidentally" brushing his hand against your thigh or by trying to get far too close early in the relationship? Does he put you in compromising situations full of temptation? Or, does he respect and protect you by making sure that he's following Ephesians 5:3:

> But among you there must not be even a hint of sexual immorality, or of any kind of impurity, or of greed, because these are improper for God's holy people.

A Christian bad boy cannot be a godly man because he does not protect his Christian sister by doing what's best for her. He's still looking out for numero uno. He does not truly love, as in 1 Cor. 13, and, therefore, cannot truly love you as Christ loves the Church and gave Himself up for her (Eph. 5:25).

Some women out there might be thinking, "But we have so much chemistry, he's so fun and exciting." I used to think the exact same thing but what Christ has taught me is: Chemistry isn't what keeps a marriage strong for 20+ years. Godliness is what keeps a couple loving each other, sacrificing for each other, and glorifying God with their marriage. A godly man leads his girlfriend or wife towards godliness, protects her heart and body, provides for her, disciples her, sacrifices himself for her, and cultivates the work of God in her. This is the kind of man to date and marry, not the bad boy who uses you for his own gain, leads towards ungodliness, blurs the boundaries that protect, and avoids wise counsel.

I used to think that if I gave up the exciting bad boy type that God would have me marry a boring, godly type. But I assure you, godly is NOT boring. Just because a guy isn't a bad boy doesn't make him a stick in the mud, goody two-shoes, but it DOES point to Christ being his heart's desire. It doesn't mean that you can't feel a strong connection with them, look lovingly in their eyes, and get butterflies when they come near, or even have a huge crush on them years down the road. I was blessed to marry a godly man who's my best friend, who's exciting, and whom I simply adore (and will for the next 50+ years). God has your best in mind and if you make His radical standards your standards, and if it's His will for you to marry, He will send you a man who will be a wonderful, lifelong companion, who you can trust, who will sacrifice himself for you, and with whom you can honor God together.

Questions That Make You Go "Hmmm"

1. What have you found most attractive about "Bad Boys'? What do you think Scripture says about those qualities?

2. What are some biblical characteristics in a guy that the Bible says are good for you?

3. Why do you think God wants you to avoid dating bad boys and date biblical boys?

4. How will what you have read change the way you choose guys?

10

Why we love Jerks

GABRIELLE PICKLE

"Is she crazy?" I shouted at the television in total exasperation. "Women can act so stupid. The moment our hearts get involved, we flip the stupid switch!" There was an old spy movie playing on TV and the woman of questionable sanity was the girlfriend of a criminal. Of course, she refused to admit that he actually was a criminal because he wasn't all bad and she loved him. When the authorities confronted her with proof of his many girlfriends, she denied it, saying, "No, he truly loves me. There is no one else. He can't leave his wife because of their kids, but he does love me." The authorities help her and her family to escape harm by putting them into witness protection. But she cannot stand being away from the man she loves. So she leaves witness protection, endangering her family, to meet up with the criminal. When the two are reunited, he tries to kill her because she is the only witness. The authorities intervene, arrest the criminal and save her life. But rather than thanking them she attacks one of the officers, enraged because they separated her from her boyfriend. She ignored unfaithfulness, criminal activities and his attempt to end her life, all because she loved him.

And as crazy as that girl seems, I can relate. No, I've never dated a criminal, but I have been that girl who ignored unbiblical behavior, rationalized red flags away and scratched things off my "list" because the object of my emotional attachment didn't have those qualities.

As women, when our hearts get involved, we tend to lose all sense of logic. We all know of, or have ourselves been, the girl who dates the cheaters, the beaters and the jerks. But she sticks with him because she loves him. She tells herself that he has such potential, she can help him change, and then she believes her own lies because she is emotionally connected to him.

Why is this? With the love of a girl comes unwavering trust. God created you, as a woman, to be the helpmeet of man, which involves supporting him in the face of great odds and trusting him above all else. There is nothing more empowering to a man than the unwavering belief and support of his wife. A respected marriage counselor observed that, "a man will usually not rise above the level at which his wife respects him." The love, trust and support of a woman is a good thing – it is designed by God to strengthen the marriage relationship. The problem is that females often give themselves emotionally to a man before marriage is even mentioned. This is one of the reasons why Scripture stresses the importance of guarding the heart. *Above all else, guard your heart, for it is the wellspring of life* (Prov. 4:23).

I quickly learned, after watching friend after friend fall prey to destructive relationships with jerks, that when you are dating a jerk you often don't see it or can't admit it. Since jerks don't walk around wearing signs, God has given us the profile of a jerk in Psalms and Proverbs.

PROFILE OF A JERK... PROVERBS CALLS HIM A FOOL

- He doesn't fear God. – Psalm 53:1

- He is arrogant, ignoring the instruction, teaching and counsel of godly people. – Proverbs 1:7

- He is complacent (not convicted) by the sin in his life. – Proverbs 1:32

- His words cannot be trusted (because of lies, slander and gossip). – Proverbs 10:8, 10, 14, 18; 18:6-7

- He does not honor his parents. – Proverbs 10:1, 15:5, 15:20, 17:21, 17:25

- He laughs at sin, it is amusing to him. – Proverbs 11:29

- He is reckless and careless. – Proverbs 14:16

- He has a quick temper and argues over anything. – Proverbs 14:17, 20:3

- He does not learn from his mistakes. – Proverbs 17:10

- He has lots of opinions, but they are not founded on the wisdom of Scripture. – Proverbs 18:2

- He trusts in himself. – Proverbs 28:26

Reclaiming Your Heart

If you read the above list and realized that you are dating, living with, engaged to, in love with, or have a crush on a guy who fits in this category of a jerk, then the Bible is very clear. If you are not married to him, you need to end the relationship. Period. If this guy is not running after Christ in his own life, then he is not God's plan for you right now. Soon he will begin to pull you down to his level, if he hasn't already. *Do not be deceived: bad company ruins good morals* (1 Cor. 15:33). He may call himself a Christian, a Bible study leader, or a member of a church staff – but if his life does not honor God, you should not be with him.

If you are the girl who is smitten with a jerk, believe me, I can empathize with the panic that is welling up in your throat as you read these Scriptures. I know that the very thought of ending things with the guy makes you sick to your stomach. I know that you cannot fathom how you'll cope or what your future would be like without him. But by asking you to end this relationship, God is trying to spare you, His precious daughter, from a great deal of heartache and painful consequences in the future. Proverbs warns of what will happen to someone who is the companion of a fool – they will get hurt. *Whoever walks with the wise becomes wise, but the companion of fools will suffer harm* (Prov. 13:20). Obey now and trust God to heal your broken heart.

GUARDING YOUR HEART

Obviously, we as females automatically trust the man we have an emotional connection with – whether or not his actions and character have earned that trust. So the wisest course of action, as a girl seeking God, is to guard our hearts against emotional attachment until he has proven himself a wise and godly guy. How do we protect ourselves from loving and trusting a guy who isn't good for us? What does guarding your heart look like? Scripture gives us some helpful guidelines.

1. BE CONTENT WHERE GOD HAS YOU.

The girl who is content with where God has her in life, who is content in her singleness, is not vulnerable to the emotional persuasion of foolish boys who wander through her life. But the girl who doesn't trust God's goodness, who doesn't wait on God's timing, or is controlled by feelings of incompleteness without a man in her life – that girl ignores red flags, lowers her standards, justifies a lack of godliness, and in the end gets hurt by the very man she wanted to love her.

In her book *Fearlessly Feminine*, Jani Ortlund says, "I am sometimes tempted to think that if God were really good,

He would grant me my heart's desire for a relationship because, of course, He wants me to be happy. But God is not good because He fulfills my desires. He is good because He is fulfilling His desires, and His desires are good for you and me. Goodness is His very nature."[1] As Christian girls, we must trust in God's goodness, *You are good and what you do is good* (Ps. 119:68). Trust that He has a plan for your current singleness. Trust that he has a plan for your life.

Leslie Ludy says, "Finding a godly guy and experiencing a God-scripting, lasting love story comes down to this: Build your existence around Christ. Jesus Christ – not finding the right guy – must be the focus of your life. He must be enough, even if no earthly love story ever comes your way. God may have given you the desire for a beautiful earthly romance, but remember to continually give that dream back to Him."[2]

2. SURROUND YOURSELF WITH WISE COUNSELORS/FRIENDS.
The girl who surrounds herself with godly friends and wise counselors will not be deceived by the smooth words and impressive gestures of foolish boys. Proverbs tells us that in an abundance of counselors there is safety (Prov. 11:14). It is not enough just for her to have wise friends, she must also heed their advice. When they tell her that a guy seems shady – that his words don't match his actions – she must listen.

3. HOLD OFF ON EMOTIONAL INVOLVEMENT.
The girl who is serious about guarding her heart (Prov. 4:23) protects herself from getting emotionally connected to a man until his character has proved him to be godly. She refrains from flirtatious behavior, talking about marriage

---

1   Jani Ortlund. *Fearlessly Feminine*, Colorado Springs, CO: Multnomah Books (2000).

2   Eric and Leslie Ludy. *When God Writes Your Love Story*, Colorado Springs, CO: Multnomah Books (2004).

too soon and spending excessive time alone with him. She observes his character and makes an objective decision before her heart gets involved. She studies Scripture to know what a godly man looks like and commits to the Lord that she will not cultivate a relationship (in her head or in her life) with anyone who does not match those criteria.

PROVERBS PAINTS A CLEAR PICTURE OF THE WISE, GODLY GUY.

- A wise man holds his temper. – Proverbs 29:11

- A wise man listens to advice and seeks the counsel of other wise men. – Proverbs 12:15, 9:8

- A wise man honors his parents, even if they are not following God. – Proverbs 15:20

- A wise man is a peacemaker. – Proverbs 16:14

- A wise man learns from mistakes and receives instruction humbly. – Proverbs 21:11

- A wise man is full of moral strength. – Proverbs 24:5

- A wise man trusts in the wisdom of the Lord, not in himself. – Proverbs 28:26

- A wise man keeps himself away from strife (aka DRAMA). – Proverbs 20:3

- A wise man has good sense and uses it. – Proverbs 16:22

- A wise man seeks wisdom, knowledge and understanding. – Proverbs 15:2, 14

- A wise man is patient and forgiving. – Proverbs 19:11

- A wise man fears the Lord and turns away from evil. – Proverbs 14:16

So, why do we love jerks?

Because jerks – boys who Proverbs calls a fool – do and say things to establish an emotional bond quickly, before their true nature is known. They make emotional promises that are not theirs to keep and in doing so sweep girls with unguarded hearts off their feet. And once the emotional connection is there, very little can make her leave the fool… because she loves him.

Just because there have been fools in your past does not mean there cannot be a wise man in your future. But you must cut off ties with fools and surround yourself with wise, godly people. Because *whoever walks with the wise becomes wise* (Prov. 13:20). It's been said that, "A woman's heart should be so hidden in God that a man has to seek Him just to find her."

QUESTIONS THAT MAKE YOU GO "HMMM"

---

1. Think about the guys you usually date: Are they what Proverbs calls wise or are they foolish?

2. What foolish quality can you replace with a wise quality next time you date a guy?

3. List the Top 5 Wise Qualities you would want in a guy? Can you list the Top 5 Foolish Qualities you would not want in a guy?

4. What makes the decision about who you date? Is it Scripture/God or is it your feelings/chemistry?

11

A Match made by My Own Making

SARAH BUBAR

As women in today's culture, we are assaulted by lessons in manipulation. We can't escape it. It's everywhere we turn. It's in that catchy song on the radio singing, "I won't stop until that boy is mine!" It's found in our favorite comedic line in a movie, "The man may be the head, but the woman – she is the neck, and she can turn the head any way she wants to."

But no matter how loudly our society advocates its barrage of manipulation tactics, there is nothing new under the sun. We aren't the first to come up with the idea. In fact, this trend has been around since Genesis and the Old Testament.

SARAH AND ABRAHAM (GENESIS 16)

We all know the story. Abraham is promised by God that he will be a great nation with descendents that outnumber the stars in the sky. Probably imagining three sets of triplets, Sarah wonders how all this is going to happen as she is unable to bear children. But little does she know that God's ways are not always our ways. As time swiftly progresses and the chances of her producing an heir are fading, Sarah begins to take matters into her own hands. She begins to take up God's rightful role in her life. Since God isn't producing an heir like He said He would, SHE WOULD! She is woman, hear her ROAR! I can almost see Sarah just picking up the reins to the situation. "Fine, if He's not going to make it happen, I can! I've got Hagar my maid. SHE can produce an heir with Abraham. I will use her to get what I want even if God isn't allowing it to happen like it should happen. I can make my own life." And like a stubborn bull, she forges ahead outside of God's protection and perfect plan. In the end, God *does* fulfill his promise to Sarah and Abraham. They *do* miraculously bear a child – one child – Isaac from whom the entire nation of Israel descends. And yet, I wonder… How different would our *world* be if Sarah had obeyed and Ishmael never had been born?

Does manipulative sin only affect **you** *or does it also affect those around you or those coming after you?*

TAMAR AND JUDAH (GENESIS 38)

Their story is a scandalous tale, the likes of which Maury Povich would love to get his hands on. There is one bad decision made after another in this narrative. On one side, you have a father-in-law shirking his God-given duties to his daughter-in-law, Tamar, for fear that his youngest son would meet the same peril as his brothers. On the other side is the forsaken daughter-in-law, Tamar, left to fend for herself in the world because her cowardly father-in-law refuses to listen to God. But, instead of resting in the protection of God, Tamar manipulates herself into an incestuous relationship in order to cling to the status she has been promised. She tricks Judah, her father-in-law, and bears his child. It's hard to know which finger to point where in this story because both parties aren't necessarily faultless. Part of you empathizes with Judah not wanting to see the death of yet another son while Tamar, the possible black widow, still lives. However, it's not like it's Tamar's fault that her husbands keep dying. She looks to Judah for godly leadership only to walk away empty handed. Yet, does that justify her deceit and manipulative behavior? Scripture does hold Tamar as more righteous than Judah, but we must see that it does not condone the sinful method she used to get there.

Is it ever right…to do wrong…to do right?

BATHSHEBA AND DAVID (2 SAMUEL 11)

Theirs is a regretful saga that ends in the death of two innocent people. There is some debate as to whether or not Bathsheba played a partnering role in this relationship or if she was merely a victim of King David's abuse of power and lustful passions. Scripture is clear that David looked on *her*. David inquired about *her*. David "took" *her*. What is unclear is what *took* actually implies. Where *took* denotes a possible force in English, in Hebrew it can also mean *to buy, acquire,* and even *marry*. Couple this definition with the fact that there is an actual word for rape used elsewhere (2 Sam. 13:14); and one can conclude that if David had actually raped Bathsheba, Scripture would have probably been clearer. What is equally noteworthy in this debate is the next phrase "when she came to him." This leads me to believe that Bathsheba and David were equally caught up in the excitement of a forbidden moment and both were scheming to keep their sin hidden from the world. Both suffered the tragic consequences of their sin, as God exposed it to their world through the prophet Nathan and they lost their baby. Sure they ended up with each other, and Bathsheba may have been the famous narrator of Proverbs 31. But was it worth it? If we could interview them now, I can guarantee they would take back that one choice they spent months manipulating away.

After all, do the ends really justify the means?

Every single one of these stories has a thread of manipulation entwined within it. All of these women came to a crossroads in their lives. Down one road was trusting God regardless of the outcome; down the other was a plan, a concrete course of action that they could make happen. And they thought they knew what was good for them better than God did.

ISAAC AND REBEKAH (GENESIS 24)

We all know Rebekah wasn't perfect by any means. In fact, there was a time later in her life when it came to her favorite son and she might have been running for Mayor of Manipulationville (Genesis 27). But when it comes to her relationship to her husband, there is a beautiful love story of divine appointment. Genesis 24 is a pretty amazing chapter, and Gabby has taken the time to really dive into it in other chapters. One thing that I find fascinating is that their story is told twice, verbatim. And if something is in God's Word *once*, it's important. But if it's in there *twice*, God is making a point. As I read over this chapter, one major thought jumps off the pages. **It was a God-thing!** From start to finish, God was orchestrating this relationship to come about. The way Isaac's servant prayed *so specifically* for her, and the way that God in turn *so specifically* answered that prayer, even her brother, Laban, upon hearing the news said, "The matter comes from the Lord; so we cannot speak to you bad or good." The servant's response was, "Do not delay me, since the Lord has prospered my way." And when Rebekah was asked if she would leave her family and marry a man she had never met, she said, "I will go." *ALL* were convinced. It was a GOD-THING.

What about your story? Are you allowing God to do HIS WILL and to take over your love life or are you manipulating the events to make them happen? How many times a week do you stalk his Facebook? How often do you allow yourself to reminisce about your most recent encounter with him? How often do you "happen" to run into him? When I was in college I remember making sure I was checking my mail at the same time this guy was checking his. I knew he'd check it after work and then head down to the cafeteria. And even if I checked it earlier that afternoon with friends, I always randomly showed up there at 5:30 checking my mail, and if we "happened" to walk down to the cafeteria together then "great." If we "happened" to wait in line together then "lucky me." If we "happened" to eat together then "he totally likes me." I was trying so hard to make something happen that I *thought* should happen. I wasn't allowing it be a God-thing. I was taking control and manipulating a relationship.

If you're orchestrating a relationship, it is no longer a God-thing. It is now a YOU-thing. If you're orchestrating a relationship, what kind of legacy are you leaving to your children? When you're old and gray and your grandchildren are snuggled up around you which phrase would you rather hear coming out of your mouth? "Hey kids, let grandma tell you how I manipulated your grandpa into marrying me." Or "Hey kids, let grandma tell you the marvelous way God worked in radically bringing your grandfather and me together." I know I would rather hear the latter.

If you manipulate your relationship into existence, who is really in control of your life? And what is your manipulation saying about your view of who God is? Does it say that He doesn't really care? Does it say that He isn't paying attention to what is going on in your life, or that you know better than He does? That He isn't fair? When I am tempted to think this way, I am reminded immediately of Psalm 139 and how God orchestrated my days before a single one of them was in existence. God has a perfect plan for your life. I am reminded of Luke 12:7, "Indeed, the very hairs of your head are all numbered. Do not fear; you are more valuable than many sparrows." Honestly, if God knows something as inconsequential as how many hairs are on my head, surely He knows if I am to marry and who I am to marry. *Surely.*

If you make your relationship happen, when it crashes all around you, who is to blame? There is safety in the perfect will of God. It is a safety that God guarantees to those who remain surrendered. Trust God with your heart, and you will not be put to shame. He has your best interest in mind. So often the problem is we confuse "our best interest" with "what I think is best." They are not one and the same. Many times what *I deem* as best is truly the worst thing for me. As my heavenly Father, He knows this, and seeks my good ALL THE TIME for He is good ALL THE TIME. But most of all, He has a passion for you, a love that sent His Son to the cross.

He loves you always.

Always.

QUESTIONS THAT MAKE YOU GO "HMMM"

1. Has there ever been a time when you've done something wrong with the hope that the ends would justify the means? How did it turn out?

2. Look real hard at your dating tendencies: Are there any ways that you have tried to manipulate a situation with a guy? Tried to make your own match?

3. Who is usually in control of your crushes, your dating, your relationships? Is it God or You?

4. How does a girl who is radically living for the Lord handle a crush?

12

Mr. Right or Mr. Right in front of you?

GABRIELLE PICKLE

Being single is not easy.

Part of the reason is because there is so much pressure to pair up and live happily ever after.

THERE IS PRESSURE FROM FRIENDS AND FAMILY:

Although married people don't help, with all their pitying looks and efforts to set you up, family can be by far the worst. Comments like "maybe you're not trying hard enough" and "better find him quick – your clock is tickin" so loud I can hear it," can make a happily-single girl consider marrying the next guy that walks along… just to end the inquisition!

THERE IS PRESSURE FROM THE WORLD:

You can't escape it…no matter where you look there are ads targeting the single crowd telling them that they would be happier in a relationship. There is an entire industry devoted to helping singles find "the one" for a price. Books like *He's Just Not that into You*, *Be Your Own Matchmaker* by millionaire matchmaker Patti Sanger, and *Crash Course in Love* by celebrity matchmakers Steve and Joanne Ward coupled with relationship websites like eHarmony, Match. com, and Chemistry.com all point to signs that the world thinks the single person could be happier. I am not saying that these things are wrong, but they are evidence that our world often views singleness as a problem.

THERE IS PRESSURE FROM OURSELVES:

The vast majority of females desire to be in a relationship with their male counterpart and to have children. These are natural, God-given desires that are not wrong. Single women look around them and see unfit teenagers getting pregnant and silly college freshmen getting married and wonder, "What is wrong with the world that those ill-equipped girls get what I want? I am emotionally, physically and financially able to be a wife and mother ... why am I not the one getting married?!!"

A world of romantic comedies and emotional tales of true love leave single girls pulling out their hair and screaming, "Where is The One?!!" And for the single girl who really does want to be married, it is easy to get discouraged. In case you haven't noticed – there are a lot of strange guys out there. The most awkward and depressing place for a single woman is a single's ministry in a local church. It is easy to turn to lost friends from work for companionship, rather than enduring the loneliness of one more Friday night eating a Lean Cuisine with Ben and Jerry. Why wait for God's Mr. Right when Mr. Right-in-front-of-you is sitting in the next office? He doesn't have any major vices, he seems like an all around good guy. So what if he's not only a CEO in work, but a CEO in church ... as in "Christmas and Easter Only'? So what if he is not involved in church, he is sort of spiritual and seeking ... something? So what if he drinks a little too much or makes fun of "Jesus Freaks," he is the life of the party? So what if he doesn't love Jesus, as long as he makes you feel loved?

So what?

THE BIBLE IS WHAT.

God is very clear on this subject of close relationships between believers and unbelievers. 2 Corinthians 6:14 says, *"Do not be unequally yoked with unbelievers."* This verse applies to all types of relationships with non-Christians, but there is only one relationship that if "yoked" with an unbeliever, cannot be undone ... Marriage. What does Paul mean by unequally yoked? The expression "unequally yoked" comes from Leviticus 19:19 and Deuteronomy 22:10, where it means "mismatched," referring to the yoking of oxen and donkeys, which would require two dissimilar creatures to walk at the same pace and to act as one in the same work. In the original Greek this verse expresses the idea of "stop being unequally yoked and work hard to not be unequally yoked at any time." Paul is warning the Corinthians against compromising the integrity and public witness of their faith. He emphasizes avoiding any action that would cause believers to link up with the world, which includes, but is not limited to, marriage.

You may think you have a lot in common with an unbeliever, or that the "lost, but so amazing" guy you are dating is the only one who really "gets" you. But if you do not have Christ in common, you have no foundation for a relationship of any kind. Paul emphasizes this with 5 rhetorical questions in the verses that follow his "unequally yoked" ultimatum.

> For what partnership has righteousness with lawlessness? Or what fellowship has light with darkness? What accord has Christ with Belial? Or what portion does a believer share with an unbeliever? What agreement has the temple of God with idols?
>
> (2 Cor. 6:14-16)

Each question demands the answer, "none at all!" And just as the answers to these five questions are clearly obvious, so the response to a believer being unequally yoked with an unbeliever should be "absolutely not!" Paul links unbelievers with lawlessness, darkness and now Satan himself. Each question contrasts negative and positive opposites to emphasize the difference between those who do know Christ as Savior and those who do not. Ultimately, they have nothing in common. And any wife married to an unsaved man will attest to this fact.

You may think that there is no harm in hanging out with your new super-cute non-Christian date night after night and weekend after weekend, but the Bible says otherwise. In 2 Corinthians 6:16–7:1 of the unequally yoked passage, Paul quotes four verses from the Old Testament to tell us why it is SO important that we not be unequally yoked with unbelievers. *For we are the temple of the living God ....* Remember how holy God considered the Temple back in the Old Testament? People could not enter into the Holy of Holies for fear of DEATH! God's Spirit literally dwelt in the Temple. Paul applies that same standard of holiness to the believers at Corinth, who were the new temple of God. They should not be unequally yoked with unbelievers because they are the TEMPLE OF GOD. Paul combines Ezekiel 37:27 and Leviticus 26:12 and both verses reference God's covenant to His chosen people, Israel. Paul sees these ancient promises as being fulfilled by believers under the new covenant. He then recites Isaiah 52:11 and Ezekiel 20:34, which speak of God calling His people to live like people of God, even in exile. Paul uses these verses to emphasize the positive action required of the Corinthian believers; they must separate themselves from anything unclean and free themselves from relationships resulting in unholy compromise. Paul is not saying that believers should withdraw from culture, but that in their pursuit of holiness they break any ties with the world that compromise the holiness of God's temple. This would include close friendships, business partnerships, peer groups, dating relationships, and yes, even marriage. It is in the generality of Paul's command that the depth and breadth of holiness expected by God is seen.

Being married to an unbeliever is hard. One woman shared her own experience, "Many Christian women who think about getting married to someone who doesn't have a place for Jesus in their lives, can't see the harm, if the man they love is morally upright. I saw no problem. But I ended up paying a heavy price in personal loneliness, marital discord, and, worst of all, disruption to my own fellowship with God." So it makes sense that some women are tempted to throw in the towel and give up. But this passage does not allow women to stop being "unequally yoked" with their unbelieving husbands. Marriage is the only "unequally yoked" relationship that cannot be broken. By quoting Old Testament passages about God's covenant with Israel in 2 Corinthians 6:16-18, Paul is emphasizing that the same ethical standards that applied in the Old Testament also apply to this issue in the New Testament. The Old Testament clearly emphasizes the finality of marriage in the eyes of God (Gen. 2:24, Mal. 2:14-16). So, 2 Corinthians 6:14–7:1 is speaking of a preventative standard in regards to marriage and not of divorce, which is supported by Paul's own teachings in 1 Corinthians 7:1-16, where he tells believers to stay with their unbelieving mate.

And so, while it can be very tempting to befriend, date and marry Mr. Right-in-front-of-you, who just so happens to be lost, God has a much better plan for you in a godly, Christian, Mr. Right. God is not being mean by commanding you to not be unequally yoked with unbelievers. He is calling you to live a holy life and He is trying to protect you, His daughter, from a great deal of heartache.

- Will an unbeliever understand that you will always love Jesus more than you love him?

- Will an unbeliever understand the necessity of your time alone with Jesus every day?

- Will an unbeliever understand when you make decisions based on Scripture rather than personal gain?

- Will an unbeliever have a problem with you giving away 10 percent of your income to church in tithe?

- Will an unbeliever agree with you on how to raise and discipline your children? Will an unbeliever want his children to grow up in church?

- Will an unbeliever want to celebrate Christmas and Easter the same way you will?

- Will an unbeliever understand God's plan for marriage and not defile it with pornography or unfaithfulness?

- When you cannot participate in sinful behavior, will he think you are rejecting him?

The most important thing in your life is foolishness to him... Your Jesus is FOLLY to him (1 Cor. 1:22-25). This passage says that as a believer, your primary influences should be believers. Your best friends should be believers. The people you get advice from should be believers. The people you date should be believers. The man you marry must be a believer! If your primary influences are unbelievers, you will be constantly tempted to sin, which goes against 2 Timothy 2:22. You will be viewed by the world as an unbeliever, simply because of who you associate with, 1 Peter 1:14-15. It is not a complicated command, but when you are the only single in your church and desperately lonely, it can feel impossible. But it is not. Pray and ask God for godly friends (I do this every time I move and have many fabulous godly brothers and sisters in Christ). Find places in the church and community to serve others (several of my friends met their spouses working at church camp, VBS and on mission trips). Enjoy your singleness: (spend this time building your relationship with God and pursuing the holiness He has called you to).

It is tempting to settle for a great lost guy over the socially-awkward stalker in the single's ministry or being alone for another Friday night. But it doesn't matter how sweet, handsome or dynamic the guy is – if he is lost then he is not God's will for you. God is not punishing you with singleness. God loves you. He wants the best for you, His daughter. For some girls, God's best for them is to be married earlier, so that they can learn important lessons about God through marriage. For other girls, God's best for them is keeping them single right now, so they can learn those same lessons through singleness. Singleness is not a problem to be fixed, the Bible says that it is God's will that everyone be single for a time and some be single forever – and those are blessed! (1 Cor. 7:32-35).

I've always known that dating a lost guy was not an option – my Dad made it very clear. And while I heeded his advice, I didn't fully understand why it was so important. Until I had a front row seat in watching someone I love fall for a non-believer. It was the most heartbreaking thing I've ever seen – a love that could never be fulfilled. Ultimately, the choice had to be made... the unbeliever or obeying God? The right choice was ultimately made, but the emotional cost was so high. I still burst into tears after a phone conversation with my loved one.

Please, please don't give your heart to anyone whose heart hasn't first been given to God!

QUESTIONS THAT MAKE YOU GO "HMMM"

1. Have you dated a non-believer?

2. How can you learn to trust God's will for not dating unbelievers?

3. If you date a non-believer, how do you think your priorities will match up? Who will guide him and grow him as a person and what will guide you? Are they the same?

SECTION 4

What You Do on the Date:

Purity

13

Sexual Purity means using Protection

Diane Montgomery

When it comes to premarital sex what are you told today? Media, peers, parents, and schools tell you, "just make sure you use protection." Guess what? God says the same thing, but for completely different reasons and in completely different ways. The world tells you to use protection so when you do choose to have sex you might not have to suffer the physical consequences, such as pregnancy or disease. But God's protection is different. It isn't a pill you can take the morning after or in a box you can buy at Wal-Mart.

His protection does not just save your body but it saves your heart a lot of pain, along with your future spouse's. So what is God's kind of protection? What does God say about preserving ourselves for purity?

Let's take a look at what He has to say in His Word.

1. Preserve yourself for holiness.

It is God's will that you should be sanctified: that you should avoid sexual immorality; that each of you should learn to control his own body in a way that is holy and honorable, not in passionate lust like the heathen, who do not know God; and that in this matter no one should wrong his brother or take advantage of him. The Lord will punish men for all such sins, as we have already told you and warned you. For God did not call us to be impure, but to live a holy life. Therefore, he who rejects this instruction does not reject man but God, who gives you his Holy Spirit.

(1 Thess. 4:3-8)

The body is not meant for sexual immorality, but for the Lord, and the Lord for the body. Flee from sexual immorality. Every other sin a person commits is outside the body, but the sexually immoral person sins against his own body.

(1 Cor. 6:13, 18, 20)

God has said, be holy because HE is holy (1 Pet. 1:13). God can only be in the presence of holiness and purity, that's why He sent His son to die for us so that we can live with Him and be declared righteous when we believe in His son. But when you say "God, I'm going to ignore your commands to avoid sexual immorality and instead I'm going to do what my boyfriend and I want to do," you are rejecting God and sinning against your own body. God says to flee from sexual actions outside of marriage because it is not good for you. He desires that you be holy because it is what's best for you, and holiness never brings heartache or pain to you and others.

2. PROTECT YOUR REPUTATION AND THE GOSPEL

Then they can train the younger women to love their husbands and children, to be self-controlled and pure… So that no one will malign the word of God.

(Titus 2:4-5)

Do you not know that your body is a temple of the Holy Spirit, who is in you, whom you have received from God? You are not your own.

(1 Cor. 6:19)

The Titus women were to teach other younger women how to be godly, how to live in such a way that no one could say anything bad about them and the Word of God. Self-control and purity are signs of a godly woman, of a woman set apart for Christ. She loves her Lord so much that she would rather live a holy, pure life than give in to temptations that only promise temporary pleasure because she wants no one to be able to say anything bad about God's children or God's Word.

We, as Christians, are set apart from the world; we are to look and act differently from them. We are to reflect Christ and the Holy Spirit within us. Like it or not, the world is constantly watching what you do, to see if you act in a way that's different than them. You declare yourself a Christian but do you act in the same ways, do the same things, and go to the same places as those who do not know Christ? Why should they want to love and obey the same God as you if you don't love and obey God's commands? What they think about you is what they'll think about God. You are not your own, you are His, and therefore you should honor His temple.

Live in such a way that is above reproach so that there is not even a hint of sexual immorality in your lives. If that means, as a couple never being alone so Christ is glorified, so be it! If that means always keeping a door open if you're in each other's rooms so the Gospel is not maligned because of that, so be it! If that means waiting to kiss or hold hands for months after dating so no one can accuse you of any immorality but instead want to know who your Lord and Savior is, then so be it! What it comes down to is, which do you love more: yourself or Christ and His Gospel; which saves souls for eternity including yours?

3. PROTECT YOUR BROTHER IN CHRIST

> But I say to you that everyone who looks at a woman with lustful intent has already committed adultery with her in his heart.
>
> (Matt. 5:28)

Jesus gives this command to men not to check out women. I used to think that guys are SUPPOSED to check out girls, it's only natural for them. But according to Jesus Christ, it's the same as them committing adultery in their hearts against their future wife and it's a sin. But what does that have to do with us?

If you knew you could save someone in your family a lot of heartache and trouble, would you try as hard as you can to do so? Why would you not do the same for your spiritual brother? Well, I know it can be weird to think about, but the guy you date, if he's a Christian, is your brother in Christ. He is a part of your Christian family. You can protect him by not purposefully dressing in a way that will make him look at you with lust. A daughter of the King does not intentionally want guys to look at her so that they sin in their hearts. A daughter of the King instead cares for her brother in Christ by dressing in a way that does not cause him to sin but instead lifts him and glorifies God.

Protecting your brother not only happens when you dress in a God-honoring manner but also when you act in a way that does not cause him to stumble sexually. He could be pressuring you to do certain things and you are going along with him, or you could be pressuring him. Either way you are not protecting him and you're not protecting his future wife. You don't know for sure if you both are meant to be together but you do know that he has a future wife. How awful would it be if someday you have to tell the wife of every one of your boyfriends what activities you both did with each other behind closed doors? Live in such a way that you have nothing to be ashamed of because you cared enough about your brother in Christ to protect him from that.

4. PRESERVE YOURSELF FOR YOUR INTENDED SPOUSE

> His left hand is under my head and his right hand embraces me. O daughters of Jerusalem, I charge you: Do not arouse or awaken love until it so pleases.
>
> (Song 8:3-4)

His left hand is under her head? His right hand embraces her? This bride in Song of Songs is now with her beloved, her husband. In a way, he's snuggling her as his wife. She knows the joy of having been pure and now the beauty of God's intended plan for purity. She is with her husband and is begging her sisters to not awaken love until it (God) desires, which is after marriage.

God desires the best for you and only does good to His children so when He says, "Do not awaken love until it so desires, flee and avoid sexual immorality." Sex outside of God's will only brings hurt to you and others. God is saying, "My daughter, I have something beautiful and wonderful intended for you, if only you will follow my ways and stay pure because sex the way I intended it is only truly enjoyable within marriage." He will NEVER withhold good from you; and if you trust God, He'll lead you down the right path and take care of you.

My husband waited eight years to kiss his future wife because he knew that every girl he dated was potentially someone's wife, but he didn't know if any of these were going to be his future spouse, and he didn't want to kiss another man's wife. So when we started dating, he waited six months, until God made it clear that I was going to be his wife, to kiss me. He had saved that and he has never regretted it, but we have both regretted anything we did that did not preserve us for each other.

5. PROTECT YOUR FUTURE MARRIAGE

> Let marriage be held in honor among all, and let the marriage bed be undefiled, for God will judge the sexually immoral and adulterous.
>
> (Heb. 13:4)

The consequences of pre-marriage sexual experiences will carry over into your marriage, and you will have to deal with them. They don't just go away once you get married. The past partners, the past experiences will come into your relationship with your husband and even your marriage bed. There will be worries from both sides: "Am I good enough compared to the other people? Are they comparing me to those other people?"

The world tells you, "You need to try this person to see if you're compatible sexually or they might be the one so enjoy each other now." But God says, "Trust me, I have someone intended for you; and when you marry that person, you won't ever regret saving yourself. If you don't, when you finally do find that person, you will have wished with everything in you that you had waited and kept your marriage bed undefiled."

A wise person once told me, "You will never regret taking it too slow in relationships, but you will always regret going too fast."

God has laid out a plan in Scripture and has given you the tools to protect yourself for sexual purity. He has always promised to do good for you and to you, to save you from hurt and destruction from sin. BUT you have to follow His commands and walk in His will; anything outside His will only brings you pain and heartache. Eve started to doubt God and started to think He was holding something good back from her, when the whole time He was trying to save her from sin and wanted her and Adam to live in His presence in the most beautiful place ever created. But because she doubted God's goodness to her and disobeyed His commands, sin entered the world, and Eve now knew heartache and pain.

Do you trust the Savior who died on a cross on your behalf, or are you starting to doubt His goodness? Do you trust that He has a wonderful plan for you when He says, "wait!"? If you have doubted before and given into temptation, you probably know the pain it brings but God is saying, "Come back to me and I will give you rest. It's not too late." There is always forgiveness and grace with the Lord, no matter what you may have done in your past. He will redeem you if you let Him. If you haven't yet strayed from God's will in this area, stay strong, my sister! You will never regret it! God is not a liar; He is only goodness and love so let's trust Him in all things and His plan for us!

QUESTIONS THAT MAKE YOU GO "HMMM"

1. What do you think God's plan for sexual purity says about His feelings for you?

2. How do you think God's plan for sexual purity helps your Christian walk?

3. In what ways have you not been protecting yourself?

4. How can you start protecting the guy you're dating?

5. Accountability is a major part in succeeding with purity so how can your godly girlfriends help you in this area?

14

Looking like a Bride

Gabrielle Pickle

He saw her across the crowded market.

She was breathtaking, with big dark eyes and a sweet smile. She was on her way to the well. He was working with his father in the family business. Their eyes met. He smiled. She blushed and looked away. His heart raced long after she disappeared from view. Over the next weeks and months he watched her, until he was certain she was the one.

If this had been 2012, he would have asked her to dinner, they would have gotten to know each other in a series of dates over the next 12 months before he finally worked up the courage to pop the question. But this story is set in Israel in Biblical times. There, when a Hebrew man desired the hand of a Hebrew woman in marriage, he had to go to his father. The father of the interested man approached the father of the potential bride to discuss the high price that would be paid for her hand in marriage. Once the price was agreed upon, the smitten man was finally able to speak with the woman who had stolen his heart. He presented himself to her with plans for their future and then he would pass a cup of wine to her. That was the moment of truth for their relationship. If she drank, it symbolized her acceptance to his proposal and lifelong commitment to him. If she passed on the cup, it signified the end of the relationship.

For a long moment no one spoke, all eyes were on the potential bride, wondering what her answer would be. Would she drink and so signify the establishment of a marriage covenant? This girl who had kept herself pure for her husband, would she set herself apart for this man? She reached for the cup. An enormous smile erupted on the face of the groom. With eyes only for each other, hearts soaring, the newly betrothed couple shared the cup. Later that evening, after much celebration, the bride's price was paid and the groom left to prepare a home for their new life together.

She was now a bride, betrothed to her beloved, set apart for him alone. No other men were even considered, she was his and he was hers. She was not yet a wife, but she was legally a bride preparing for her wedding day. With the help of her mother, aunts and cousins, she made her wedding dress and put together everything she would need for her new home. She prepared by day and waited by night for her groom to come. Her dowry kept her busy while her heart longed for that moment when he would return for her and take her to himself.

He returned to his father's house to prepare the Bridal Chamber for the one his heart loved. No one knew when it would be finished, but once it was ready the groom would lead a torchlight procession, with his best man and members from the wedding party, and proceed to claim his bride. The best man would shout their arrival and the bridal party would light their lamps and join in the procession back to the father's house where the wedding would be held. There awaited a magnificent wedding feast that would last for seven days in celebration of their union.

But for now she waits, keeping herself pure for her beloved. And everyone knows she is a bride, saving herself for the one who paid a high price for her hand.

You are also a bride. If you are a Christian, your story strongly resembles the love story of the Hebrew girl above. God so loved the world – you – that He sent His only Son, Jesus, to pay the price to redeem you from sin (John 3:16-18, Eph. 5:25-27). Jesus is your bridegroom (John 3:29). Jesus paid the highest price known to man for his bride; he paid your price with his blood (Heb. 9:12). You were bought with a price, redeemed for Him alone (1 Cor. 6:19-20). Just like the young Hebrew bride, you too are asked to share in the cup of the New Covenant (Matt. 26:27-28). You are now set apart for Him alone, the Bride in preparation for her coming Bridegroom (2 Cor. 6:17). Jesus has gone to prepare a place for you, His bride, but He promises to return soon (John 14:2-3). When He comes for you everyone will know it, but no one knows the day or hour when He will come (Matt. 24:42-44). Until that glorious day, you are to prepare for His return (Luke 12:40). And you are to live in purity, so that the whole world will know that you are His (2 Cor. 11:2-3, 2 Tim. 2:22).

This is your love story.

This is why purity matters. You are the Bride of Christ, set apart from the world for Him alone. Purity is what sets you apart from the world. Purity is how the world recognizes you as the Bride of Christ. Sadly, many believers do not live or act or look like the Bride. They believe the lies of the world about purity. These lies hold them in bondage from living the victorious life of the redeemed.

LIE 1: A LIFE OF PURITY IS LAME AND BORING.
Purity is saving yourself – mind, body and soul – for only one. If that is lame and boring, why is the entire world

desperately chasing after "true love?" God is true love and only by living His way will we experience that love.

> It is God's will that you should be sanctified: that you should avoid sexual immorality; that each of you should learn to control his own body in a way that is holy and honorable, not in passionate lust like the heathen, who do not know God.
>
> (1 Thess. 4:3-5)

The world tells us to partake of sinfully delightful pleasures now, rather than choosing a life of purity. The world offers excitement followed by heartache and devastation. God offers an adventurous, purposeful life characterized by love. The world offers cheap thrills, rather than true love. The world tries to prostitute us, while God asks us to be His bride.

Would you rather be loved or used?

LIE 2: PURITY IS OLD FASHIONED AND IMPOSSIBLE IN TODAY'S WORLD.

Purity is unto the Lord, not unto the situation! Purity is not only possible today, it is commanded. God provides clear directions on how to live a life of purity, even in 2010. How can a woman keep her life pure? By the grace of God (Titus 2:11-12), by seeking God with a whole heart (Ps. 119:10), by obeying Scripture, by memorizing Scripture verses (Ps. 119:11), by not gratifying sinful desires (Gal. 5:16), and by choosing everyday to live in the Spirit (Gal. 5:17).

> Everyone will be tempted in some area of purity, but Jesus will not let you be tempted more than you can resist. "God is faithful; he will not let you be tempted beyond what you can bear...he will also provide a way out so that you can stand up under it."
>
> (1 Cor. 10:13)

Choose to flee temptation and you will find yourself running towards purity.

LIE 3: PURITY MEANS NOT HAVING SEX, BUT EVERYTHING ELSE IS OK.

Purity is not just abstaining from sexual acts, but keeping oneself from being polluted by the world (James 1:27). Purity means not participating in anything that arouses sexual emotions (2 Tim. 2:22). Anything thought, seen, read, heard, or done that cultivates lustful desire is impure. Purity affects not only what you do, but also what you think, what you allow people to say in front of you and what you watch on TV! (Matt. 5:27-30) Get rid of everything that is impure (Col. 3:5-10). Paul tells believers not to have even a hint of sexual immorality or impurity in their lives,

> But among you there must not be even a hint of sexual immorality, or of any kind of impurity, because these are improper for God's holy people.
>
> (Eph. 5:3)

You are God's holy people, redeemed from sin, so be holy in every area of your life!

LIE 4: IF I WAS MARRIED, I WOULDN'T STRUGGLE WITH PURITY.

While marriage is the God-ordained place for physical expressions of love, lust is never satisfied. Lust has emotional affairs with men other than her husband. Lust lives in a fantasy world apart from the husband who loves her. Lust is addicted to pornography. Lust experiments with the forbidden. God designed marriage to be amazing and full of love, but marriage does not fix the impure desires of unbridled lust.

Purity is not a "True Love Waits" ring given to 12 year olds that ends when they exchange it for a wedding ring at 23. Purity is a lifelong commitment. Purity means not awakening love before marriage, being faithful to one spouse, not inviting other people into the intimacy of marriage (through books, internet, TV), it means remaining pure after a spouse has passed, it means keeping your marriage bed pure at all times, it means honoring God with your body at every stage of life. Purity is a life-long pursuit.

> Let marriage be held in honor among all, and let the marriage bed be undefiled, for God will judge the sexually immoral and adulterous.
>
> (Heb. 13:4)

The happiest marriages are those committed to purity from birth til death.

LIE 5: VIRGINITY IS EMBARRASSING.

More and more Christians seemed to be ashamed of their purity. Ashamed to be the only high school senior with no experience. Ashamed to be the 29-year-old virgin at work. Ashamed to admit to bawdy friends that you don't fantasize about men other than your husband. What is there to be ashamed of? No bride is ashamed of her bride status. She shows off that ring to anyone who will stop and look! Why are believers ashamed of their purity as the Bride of Christ? Scripture commands us not to be ashamed of the gospel – it saves us. (Rom. 1:16, 2 Tim. 1:8) Purity is evidence of the gospel at work in our lives!

> Since we have these promises, dear friends, let us purify ourselves from everything that contaminates body and spirit, perfecting holiness out of reverence for God.
>
> (2 Cor. 7:1)

Live boldly as the Bride that you are!

The time had finally come…

Her wedding day was here. She heard the best man from a long way off, as he shouted over and over "Behold, the bridegroom comes! Come out to meet him!"

(Matt. 25:1-12). She slipped into her wedding gown, which was all laid out and waiting for this moment. She carefully put on her veil, a symbol of her purity before and after the wedding, and ran out to meet her beloved. With eyes full of love and hearts completely pure, both were able to say, "I am my beloved's and my beloved is mine" (Song 5:3). They were united in marriage by the light of a hundred candles, in the presence of God and witnesses.

One day, as the Bride of Christ, you too will have that experience.

> For the Lord himself will descend from heaven with a cry of command, with the voice of an archangel, and with the sound of the trumpet of God. And the dead in Christ will rise first. Then we who are alive, who are left, will be caught up together with them in the clouds to meet the Lord in the air, and so we will always be with the Lord.
>
> (1 Thess. 4:16-18)

When standing before the Lord as His Bride, don't you want to be able to say that you have pursued purity? That your life has been a steady progression from impurity to purity in the Lord? If you are a Christian, your past – no matter how ugly – has been purified in Christ if you confess those sins and repent. So, turn from the ways of the world and chase after purity!

> You are not your own; you were bought at a price. Therefore honor God with your body.
>
> (1 Cor. 6:18-20)

You are the Bride of Christ, set apart from the world for Him alone.

Live as the Bride in your singleness. Live as the Bride in your marriage.

QUESTIONS THAT MAKE YOU GO "HMMM"

1. Does your life show you to be the Bride of Christ? Why or why not?

2. Are there any ways God would want you to look more like a bride?

3. What are some impure things God would want you to get rid of?

15

It's All in Your Head:
Battling for Purity of Mind

DIANE MONTGOMERY

Jeff was the cutest, funniest guy Jenny knew and she got butterflies every time he came around. Jenny liked to think about how they'd held hands for the first time at the movies and where they had their first kiss at the park, leading to other intimate moments. He was the perfect guy for her but, unfortunately, he was in her imagination.

During vacation, Britney met Dustin who was mysterious, incredibly handsome, and not to mention, very sexy. They walked on the beach all day, talked about their hopes and dreams till the stars came out. Their vacation fling was like something out of a movie. They were meant to be .... if it wasn't all one of Britney's fantasies.

Paul and Ashley had been on three dates so far and it was going pretty well. When they weren't together, Ashley couldn't help but imagine what they'd be like as a couple. Of course they would be holding hands, getting closer on the couch during movies, and kissing...a LOT. Ashley hoped that everything she'd been imagining would come true.

Have you ever imagined your perfect boyfriend? Have you ever made up an imaginary romantic rendezvous? Have you ever envisioned a flirtatious conversation with your coworker?

We've all played mental "pretend" at one point in our lives. We've all conjured up situations or people in our minds. Sometimes it's an innocent conversation with the boy in class but sometimes it can be more sensuous thoughts you would just die if anyone knew about. But what's so wrong with "playing pretend"? If you don't do it, then what's so wrong with thinking about it? What's the big deal with mental purity?

FANTASIES AREN'T REAL

Fantasies are unreal mental images meaning they're not true. They're a lie in your mind that's being entertained, developed, and nurtured. When you make up an imaginary boyfriend, "pretend" relationship, or perfect date, you begin to make an ideal and standard that cannot be attained.

Dating shows are the perfect example of this. The women go on exotic dates filled with five star dinners, private concerts, and helicopter rides. Everything is designed to be the most picture-perfect date. But what happens when the fantasy dates disappear and they're left dating in the real world? The relationship falls apart. An unattainable ideal has been set up in their minds and everything else is a disappointment in comparison.

When you "play pretend" with dating, you're setting yourself up for relationship failure. Contemplating dating fantasies will only leave you unsatisfied, disappointed, and continually searching for the "ideal." You'll always compare every guy, every date, and every relationship to the fantasy in your mind. There will never be a guy or a relationship like the one you invented because no person or relationship is perfect.

THOUGHTS TURN INTO ACTION

Our thoughts determine our actions. So letting lustful fantasies enter your mind makes it much harder to fight lustful actions. The more impurely you think, the more

impure thoughts become okay, justifiable, and "not so bad."
Eventually, when you're confronted with real temptations
they won't seem so bad, they'll feel "ok" because you've
grown fond of them, they've become part of your life. If
impure thinking becomes a normalcy in your mind it will
eventually become a normalcy in your life. What is in your
mind will eventually overflow into your life.

> For from within, out of men's hearts, come evil thoughts,
> sexual immorality, theft, murder, adultery, greed, malice,
> deceit, lewdness, envy, slander, arrogance and folly.
>
> (Mark 7:21-22)

If you set your mind on Christ, who redeemed you from
your sinful nature, then you'll live in accordance with
Christ. Your mind will become more like His and your
actions will follow.

> Those who live according to the sinful nature have their
> minds set on what that nature desires; but those who live
> in accordance with the Spirit have their minds set on
> what the Spirit desires.
>
> (Rom. 8:5)

What you decide to set your mind on is of the utmost
importance. It determines how you will live your life and for
whom you will live. If you think like Christ, you'll act like
Christ. If you think like your flesh, you'll live like your flesh.
But you have to choose what you'll think and how you'll act.

LUSTFUL THOUGHTS ARE SINFUL THOUGHTS
Because God demands complete purity from us, He not
only wants us to keep our bodies pure but our minds as well.

> But I [Jesus] say to you that everyone who looks at
> a woman with lustful intent has already committed
> adultery with her in his heart.
>
> (Matt. 5:28)

This verse doesn't just apply to guys. We, as women, are also held to the same standard. If we look at a guy or just imagine a guy with any lust in our hearts, then we've already sinned. You may be the most physically pure person around but if you've had impure thoughts then you're guilty of sexual immorality.

> For this is the will of God, your sanctification: that you abstain from sexual immorality; that each one of you know how to control his own body in holiness and honor, not in the passion of lust like the Gentiles who do not know God.
>
> (1 Thess. 4:3-5)

Our thoughts and our actions tell others whom we follow. Those who don't know God give into the sensual desires of their flesh. But those who know God abstain from anything sexual outside of marriage, whether it's physical or mental. They know they're one of His vessels meant for holiness and God-honoring actions.

> So you also must consider yourselves dead to sin and alive to God in Christ Jesus. Let not sin therefore reign in your mortal body, to make you obey its passions. Do not present your members to sin as instruments for unrighteousness, but present yourselves to God as those who have been brought from death to life, and your members to God as instruments for righteousness.
>
> (Rom. 6:11-13)

When you choose to dwell on impure thoughts, you're presenting a vessel intended for righteousness and instead using it for sin. You choose righteous thoughts or sinful thoughts. It's up to you; are you going to be an instrument for sin or for God's glory?

LUSTFUL THOUGHTS ARE YOUR ENEMY

Believe it or not, all those fantasies, imagined boyfriends, and sensual thoughts are actually your enemies. They're not your friend but are trying to attack your soul (1 Pet. 2:11). There's a war going on, not a physical war, but a spiritual war against the flesh. And these spiritual battles first begin in our minds.

> For though we walk in the flesh, we are not waging war according to the flesh. For the weapons of our warfare are not of the flesh but have divine power to destroy strongholds. We destroy arguments and every lofty opinion raised against the knowledge of God, and take every thought captive to obey Christ, being ready to punish every disobedience, when your obedience is complete.
>
> (2 Cor. 10:3-6)

We have to battle constantly so we can conquer sin in our everyday lives. All thoughts that are contrary to Scripture must be taken captive. If we won't take them captive, then our flesh will win. They'll be in control of our actions so they no longer reflect Christ.

So how do you conquer the lustful thoughts of the flesh and transform them into godly thoughts?

First, you have to take your thoughts captive. When the enemy begins to creep into your mind, you have to be able to recognize the enemy immediately and then arrest him. This is why knowing the truth of God's Word is so important (Ps. 119:11). You need to be able to recognize truth and lies so that when thoughts about guys, relationships, or sex come into your mind, you can immediately refuse to think about them.

With the Holy Spirit's help, you can take the sensual thoughts, the imaginary relationships, and the fantasies captive, putting them to death. Only by the Spirit can you put to death everything that is according to your flesh and become alive in Christ (Rom. 8:13; Col. 3:5). This is the only way you can begin to live in righteousness and win the war against your enemy.

After you've taken the thought captive you have to begin to retrain and refill your mind with what's good, truthful, and blessed by God. You have to start thinking more like Christ if you want your life to look more like Christ. Philippians 4:8-9 shares how you can do this:

> Finally, brothers, whatever is true, whatever is honorable, whatever is just, whatever is pure, whatever is lovely, whatever is commendable, if there is any excellence, if there is anything worthy of praise, think about these things. What you have learned and received and heard and seen in me – practice these things, and the God of peace will be with you.

If you're not thinking on truth, on whatever is pure, on whatever is lovely, then the peace of God will be missing from your life. Giving in to the desires of the flesh will never fulfill you; it will only leave you feeling discontentment, emptiness, and shame. Paul asks a grim question to believers:

> But what fruit were you getting at that time from the things of which you are now ashamed? For the end of those things is death.
>
> (Rom. 6:21)

Sister, you are no longer enslaved to sin so why continue to chain yourself to sin's lustful desires? If you're a child of God, then you've been crucified with Christ. Christ has set you free from those chains of death and you're no longer a slave to sin but a slave to a righteous and merciful God, who will leave you completely satisfied and whole (Rom. 6:21-22). You have been radically changed body, soul, and MIND by a holy God. So which master will you choose to be a slave to: a God who intended a life for you that brings complete fulfillment, joy and acceptance in His love? Or sin which leaves you empty with an insatiable appetite for every fleshly desire?

How can you have purity of mind during the different stages of life?

PURITY IN SINGLENESS

While you're single, it's hard not to think about the relationship you wish you had or the guy you wish was sharing life with you. But if you're single at the moment, then that's exactly what God wills for you right now. God doesn't want you to be with someone right now for your good. So thinking about the relationship or the guy that isn't God's will for you is sin. The more you think about what you don't have, the more you'll become discontent with your life and with God.

I know imagining your perfect guy can feel good and fill a void in your life, but it's only temporary. When you wake up from dreaming, you'll feel worse. You'll only be reminded about what's not in your life at the moment. So instead of pondering on what you wish you had, think about the good things that are in your life. Think about what's true, what's good, what's excellent. Think about the friendships, family, and opportunities God has given you. You'll see that God isn't withholding good from you and He's blessed your life immensely (Ps. 84:11). What will begin to happen after you've changed the way you think, is God's peace and joy will begin to flow from your heart and you'll become more content with the life you have.

PURITY IN DATING

Keeping your thoughts true and pure during dating is perhaps the hardest feat. Everyone talks about how to keep physically pure, which is extremely important, but rarely is mental purity given the attention it's due. Keeping yourself physically pure while dating a person is hard enough, but it's even harder to keep your mind chaste too.

If you're desiring to keep your dating relationships pure then you're not doing yourself any favors by imagining what you can't do physically. You're making it harder on yourself to remain physically pure when you think about it so often, fantasizing about how nice it would be to do. You're surrounding yourself with sin, fantasizing about sexual immorality, and giving Satan a foothold in your life and relationships (Eph. 4:27).

As you begin to like a guy more and more, you start to think about him even more. You imagine what your next date will be like, how to get him to find you more attractive, and you begin to imagine what you'll do physically: sometimes it's holding hands, sometimes it's cuddling, but sometimes your thoughts begin to venture towards things that we're commanded to flee from (1 Cor. 6:18). Some even begin to plan how they can make these carnal thoughts a reality.

To battle these thoughts, find Scriptures that will help you meditate on truth when you're tempted physically and mentally. When the thoughts begin, refuse to ponder on them. Instead replace images of you and your boyfriend with images of how Christ has set you free from your bondages to sin (Titus 2:14, 1 Cor. 5:15). God has given you the Bible to help you overcome sin and help you avoid situations that aren't for your good. Use His Truth to overcome sin and move towards living the righteous and best life God intended for you.

PURITY IN MARRIAGE

You may be wondering why purity in marriage makes the list. Married people don't have to deal with sexual purity anymore right? Unfortunately, it's a battle even married women face. They don't necessarily have it easier than their single friends. It's easy to start checking out the guy working out next to you. He's so fit and your husband... well he's not so fit. It's easy to begin thinking about how much you enjoyed the conversations with your coworker the past few weeks and start figuring out how you can have more. It's easy to begin thinking about what it would be like to be intimate with another man.

If you find yourself thinking about other men, if you find yourself comparing your husband to one of your guy friends then take immediate action. Refuse to let the thought have anymore influence on you. Instead, think about the truth of God's Word, think about the good things in your husband, think about how God has blessed your life. But also remember that lustful thoughts are sin and can have dire consequences.

Entertaining fantasies when you're married is very dangerous because it can lead to affairs or complete dissatisfaction with your husband. Lustful thoughts not only damage your relationship with God but they can damage your relationship with your husband, family, and possibly end up damaging the Gospel. Are the lies, the fantasies, worth the pain and heartache you and others may go through? Is it worth putting a wedge between you and God?

You have to decide which side you're on before you go into battle. When you hold on to sexual sin, you're putting a wedge between you and your Savior. You're deciding to choose lies over truth, shame over redemption, dirtiness over purity. When you decide to say no to sexual immorality, you're choosing Christ who mercifully saved you from sin's darkness and bondage; you're choosing to live in complete satisfaction and spiritual joy with the Lord (1 Pet. 2:11, Mark 4:19).

QUESTIONS THAT MAKE YOU GO "HMMM"

1. What can you do when a tempting thought enters your mind? What can you focus on instead?

2. What do you think you need in your arsenal before you begin to fight the mental purity battle?

3. At what point do you find yourself starting to fantasize? How can you take preventative measures so it doesn't happen in the future?

4. What are some creative ways that can help you start replacing impure thoughts with Christ-centered thoughts?

SECTION 5

When the Date Ends:

Singleness

16

Oh No!
Is Singleness in my future?

Sarah Bubar

OH NO!! Is Singleness my *future*??

I lay on my bed crying my heart out to God. I had just experienced yet another heart-wrenching breakup with a man who is now my fifth ex-boyfriend, and I was devastated. This time maybe more than all the other times. This time I was the one being broken up with, I was the one not in control of whether I would be with this guy. I was the one...being dumped.

So there I was, wallowing in a pool of adverse thoughts, convinced I would never recover. Sure, singleness may have been a part of my past. And for some of us, it's even a very real part of our present. But to think that singleness is what I have to look forward to is an extremely hard concept with which to come to grips. I have to admit, I questioned what God was doing. I questioned why He had led me into this relationship[1] only to have my heart dashed on the rocks months later. Wasn't the point of all of this messiness

---

1   When I use the term *relationship*, I mean a dating relationship or a meaningful friendship where you and the guy are exclusively seeing each other within Biblical boundaries. I do not mean living together as the world would define the term relationship.

to find a husband? Unfortunately, it was several years after this low point that this radical consideration dawned on me: Sometimes, God leads us into relationships not for the purpose of getting a man, ring or children until death "does us part." Sometimes (most times, if we're really honest with ourselves), relationships are about becoming more like Christ. I told you it was radical. But, I am confident, if we can enter into a relationship with this mindset – becoming more like Christ – then, when or if it ends, it has been time well spent.

But how do you do that? How do you see God's overarching purpose in bringing you and "that guy" together when your heart is ripped from your chest when the relationship ends? How do you pick yourself up and try at it again?

By guarding your heart.

Now, before you get frustrated with the Sunday School answer that has just been handed to you as an answer to one of the most puzzling questions raised in the dating scene, let me explain what I mean.

1. GUARDING ISN'T AS MUCH ABOUT PROTECTING YOUR HEART AS IT IS ABOUT ENTRUSTING IT.

When it comes to the idea of guarding our hearts, so often we envision the duties of a point-guard blocking all passes the opponent takes to score a point, or a fortified castle impenetrable and safe. However, when Scripture talks about guarding our hearts, it talks about not allowing sin to enter into it. Proverbs 4:6 says, "Do not forsake [wisdom], and she will keep you; love her, and she will guard you." Proverbs 4 speaks to the influence sin has in our lives, its ability to cloud our decision-making process and how not to allow ungodly influences to persuade it.

So, when we guard our hearts biblically:

- It does not mean we're living atop a mighty fortress looking out over the beckoning men in fear that one of them might hurt us.

- It does not mean *we* serve as protectors; the Lord does.

But then what does it mean?

- It DOES mean we live radically for the Lord, it requires a high level of trusting on our part. Trusting that the Lord is more in control of our love life than we are, trusting that the Lord is working out His plans and purposes for our lives and using our relationships to do that, is all a key ingredient to radical dating. But how do we biblically guard our hearts and trust the Lord in our singleness?

2. GUARDING YOUR HEART MEANS YOU GUARD YOUR MIND. So many of us take our cues for love and dating from our favorite Jane Austen novel, *Sense and Sensibility*. Like Marianne who tragically has to pick the pieces of her heart off the floor after wicked Willoughby has crushed her with his sudden dismissal, we echo her words on their love: "It was implied but never declared. Sometimes I thought it had been, but it never was."[2] And so often we have these imaginary relationships with men that we've never even spoken a word to. We must be on guard to this line of thinking, this line of pretending. It will only set us up for disappointment, distrust, and disillusionment.

We must guard our thoughts! Philippians 4:4–8 tells us exactly how we are to do this:

Firstly, we are to *Rejoice! Rejoice in the Lord always; again I will say, rejoice.* Paul wasn't just suggesting "Pie in the Sky" Christianity. This was dig-down-deep, radically-inspired

---

2   quote from the film, *Sense and Sensibility* (Columbia Pictures, 1995).

rejoicing, remembering that you have been given CHRIST! So rejoice! When we are radically guarding our hearts, we can say, "Jesus means more to me than this man's affections. And if I end up with no man, I will rejoice because I have Jesus!"

Secondly, *don't be anxious, instead pray.* Philippians 4:6 and 7 says, *Do not be anxious about anything, but in everything by prayer and supplication with thanksgiving let your requests be made known to God. And the peace of God, which surpasses all understanding, will guard your hearts and your minds in Christ Jesus.* Don't speculate "He didn't ask me out. No one is ever going to ask me out!!" Instead when you find yourself worrying about the prospects dwindling around you, pray. *Pray!* When we're hurting or restless, hearing someone say, "Pray about it," can be like pouring salt on a wound. And yet when I look at Christ and His ministry to His disciples, His first line of defense in getting Peter ready for battle was prayer!

> Simon, Simon, Satan has asked to sift you as wheat. But I have prayed for you, Simon, that your faith may not fail (Luke 22:31-32).

If this was the FIRST thing Christ did for those He loved, why is it my last? Why is it after we have exhausted every other possible resource, do we *then* go to God in prayer? Paul tells us to "Be anxious for nothing, and pray about *everything!*" Bring your requests before the Lord. Entrust your cares and concerns to His capable control, and then allow the peace of God to guard your heart!

Thirdly, *keep an eternal perspective.* Paul tells us to, *Let your reasonableness be known to everyone. The Lord is at hand.* When you finally meet Christ face to face, the first thought isn't going to be "and WHY was I single the entire time?" It's going to be "I am unworthy of your grace. I should have done more for You." So realize that while your singleness may be a part of your future here on earth, your singleness will be a part of your past once you are escorted into Heaven as the Bride of Christ. Our earthly struggles we face today are going to fade into the background once we have the perspective of eternity with Christ. Remember this the next time discouragement reminds you of your marital status.

Lastly, *THINK* on these things. *Whatever is true, whatever is noble, whatever is right, whatever is pure, whatever is lovely, whatever is admirable – if anything is excellent or praiseworthy – think about such things* (Phil. 4:8). Paul gives us an exhaustive list of ideas on which to meditate, attitudes to acquire. When we actively engage in training our thought lives to focus on these things, contentment and trust in the Lord comes that much easier. Contentment no longer becomes this arduous task. Instead it is a natural overflow of the work of God in our lives.

The interesting thing is that the object of most of our desires is not evil. It's not that it's wrong to want to be married or in a relationship. Those are good and positive things. The problem comes in their growth when that once innocent desire grows to a demand. We now demand that God do this in our lives. Then that demand, unfulfilled, grows to disappointment which eventually grows to a distrust in God and ultimately can destroy your intimacy with Him.

Controlling what you think about, entrusting your desires to the Lord prayerfully, rejoicing over what the Lord has given you and keeping an eternal perspective about life all contribute to your living life in a state of true contentment, single or not.

3. GUARDING YOUR HEART ISN'T JUST ABOUT YOU.
It's also about guarding your brothers. Having older brothers, I grew up watching how girls treated my brothers, and many times it wasn't "in Christian love," but in relational manipulation. In our family we used to call it "Come, come, come. Go. Go. Go," syndrome. Girls would string them along because they liked the attention one of my brothers gave them. They were sugary-sweet to me, the younger sister, in an effort to gain family approval. And then when the relationship ended those sweet girls turned

cruel. They were NOT guarding my brothers and they were definitely not regarding them as brothers in Christ.

1 Corinthians 13 speaks to this exact issue. It was originally written to a fractious group of people who were so busy pleasing themselves, they forgot to regard one another with love, true biblical love. Love never ends, even when the relationship is over. This is the standard to which we are to aspire. But our culture is very quick to suggest that we CUT them out of our lives, have nothing more to do with them. For us Christians, we must remember that though there might be a time of separation required to heal, "cutting someone out" is not biblical love and not guarding your brother in Christ. After all, he may not be your boyfriend anymore, but he is still and forever will be your brother in Christ!

It's been ten years since that major break up happened, since I had to peel myself off my bed that day and continue on with life as I knew it...single. And those ten years haven't been all bad. In fact, they've been pretty amazing. The Lord has brought different lessons in my life that I have had to learn. He's brought some of the best friends I've ever had into my life. He's given me more ministry opportunities than I know what to do with. And He's blessed me, "exceedingly and abundantly above all I could ask or think."

Is Singleness my future? Is Singleness yours? Only the Lord knows. But in the meantime, let us be women who guard our hearts.

QUESTIONS THAT MAKE YOU GO "HMMM"

1. If singleness is to be your future, how do you feel about that?

2. What do those thoughts say about the character of God?

3. Does that reflect the reality of who you know God to be?

4. List three things about having a "single future" that could bring God glory? How can you learn to embrace these?

17

Making Sense of your Singleness

GABRIELLE PICKLE

It is a truth universally acknowledged, that a single man in possession of a good fortune, must be in want of a wife. With those famous words, Jane Austen opens the story of *Pride and Prejudice.*[1] Her renowned work unfolds the tumultuous friendship and romance of the prejudiced Elizabeth Bennet and prideful Mr. Darcy. I've read that opening line more times than I can count, yet this afternoon is the first time it made me shout with laughter… in a public coffee shop. Ms. Austen starts her book focusing on the single men who have reached a point in their lives where the next logical step is to find a wife. I just imagined if she had focused on single women, the opening line would have been quite different… *"It is a truth universally acknowledged by females of all ages, that a single girl in possession of a pulse, longs deeply for the love of a man."*

While the Mr. Darcy male types may be able to wait on love until they have all their ducks in a row, most females crave love so deeply that they don't care if the ducks are in a row, a circle or a hexagon. And there is a very good possibility that they will abandon the ducks altogether

---

1   Austen, Jane. *Pride and Prejudice.* (Dover Thrift Editions) Dover Publications, (1995).

for the mere possibility of love. The reality of femininity is that we all long to be loved. It doesn't matter our age, background, relationship past, or dress size – every female desires to be loved and cherished. The deepest desire of our heart is to be the ultimate treasure to someone.

And when we don't have that love or see it in the foreseeable future, we often react in fear, desperation, anger, and despair. Apart from living in the power of the Holy Spirit and the love of Jesus Christ the whole singleness, dating and heartbreak mess will make us crazy.

We react in several different ways:

MISERABLE CHARLOTTE:
Whether or not she admits it, she lives like God is punishing her with singleness. Terrified that if she enjoys her singleness, God will notice and smite her with singleness forever. She believes that the obvious misery and complaints over her current single state will compel God to hurry up and make her dream husband appear.

WHAT'S THE POINT LYDIA:
Not happy with her single state, Lydia tries to punish God by living her single time only for herself. Doing what she wants, when she wants it with no concern for anyone who isn't male and single. She uses and abuses the gift of single-ness so that God will know He has made a mistake with-holding a man from her.

LONELY MARY:
While she rarely uses the word "woe," a conversation with Mary will find you attending an impromptu pity party over her single state. Conversations on boys, dating and relationships all seem to end in the fact that God must not love her as much as He does her friends, cause they have husbands and she doesn't.

CATHOLIC JANE:
She lives life believing that God is holding back the perfect man until she meets some unknown level of goodness. It is like she has to prove to God that she is worthy of marriage and a husband. Singleness is a level in a Super Mario game and she has to rack up enough points to move to the next level …. aka marriage.

JUDGMENTAL CATHERINE:
She spends her days looking around at all of the immature and ill-equipped married couples around her and pitches a fit. Furious at God, she frequently demands, "How can they be married and I am not? I would make such a better wife or girlfriend than she does!"

All of these reactions to singleness are based on an anger and distrust of God. These girls not only don't understand God's plan for singleness, they also don't have a biblical perspective on marriage. God designed the marriage relationship to sanctify the husband and wife, reflect Christ's love for the church to a lost world and raise godly children (Eph. 5:22-33, Gen. 1:27-28). Singleness is a time devoted solely in service to God – physically, emotionally and spiritually (1 Cor. 7: 32-35).

If you look anywhere other than the cross of Jesus Christ to make sense of your singleness, you will be disappointed and confused. God did not make a mistake and misplace your husband. God did not orchestrate your time of singleness for you to be alone. He has brought you to this point in life to be with Him. You are single so that you can worship God with your singleness. He is giving you the once-in-a-lifetime opportunity to be single-mindedly devoted to Him. He is giving you the chance to have your heart belong solely to Him. What a sweet gift to be able to give to your Savior. Paul explains,

I want you to be free from anxieties. The unmarried man is anxious about the things of the Lord, **how to please the Lord**. But the married man is anxious about worldly things, how to please his wife, and his interests are divided. And the unmarried or betrothed woman is anxious about the things of the Lord, how to be holy in body and spirit. But the married woman is anxious about worldly things, how to please her husband.

(1 Cor. 7: 32-35)

We either devote our singleness to worshipping ourselves or worshipping our Savior. There is no in-between. **Your time of singleness – whether long or short – isn't about you. It's about God.** It is about offering up your singleness as a sacrifice of worship to your Lord.

Therefore, I urge you brethren, by the mercies of God, to present your bodies a living and holy sacrifice acceptable to God, which is your spiritual act of worship. And do not be conformed to this world, but be transformed by the renewing of your mind, so that you may prove what the will of God is, that which is good and acceptable and perfect.

(Rom. 12:1-2)

Single doesn't mean staying in every Friday night, watching reruns in the company of Ben & Jerry. You have the liberty to plan your life around God alone – make the most of it! Schedule dates with Jesus, take a prayer retreat, host a Bible study, have lunch with new church members, babysit for stay-at-home moms, disciple a college student, volunteer in the church nursery, work at a local homeless shelter, donate your disposable income to Christian ministries, or use your vacation to take mission trips.

Jane Austen knew a great deal about romantic relationships, she made her livelihood developing them on page. And perhaps it was because she was single herself that she relates so well with readers seeking a romantic story. She understood the plight of the single woman. The search for security, intimacy, companionship and love found in a man. But whether you are prideful as Mr. Darcy, prejudiced as Elizabeth Bennett, miserable as Charlotte Lucas, lonely as Mary Bennett, or judgmental as Lady Catherine deBurge, in our singleness our attitudes can not be derived from a Jane Austen novel. They must have their basis on the Word of God.

It is a truth universally acknowledged by females of all ages, that a single girl in possession of a pulse, longs deeply for the love of a man. That pulse is given by God so that we would yearn for Him. Singleness isn't something to fear but instead embrace. It's a gift from God that allows you to seek Him with your whole heart and have that deep longing fulfilled in His embrace. The time may come when God brings about a lasting marriage relationship into your life, but until that time comes, your life is still being lived. It doesn't start when that relationship does. Life starts when Christ becomes what you yearn for.

QUESTIONS THAT MAKE YOU GO "HMMM"

1. How have you reacted to your singleness? Are you Miserable Charlotte, What's The Point Lydia, Lonely Mary, Catholic Jane, or Judgmental Catherine?

2. How has your attitude towards singleness furthered the kingdom? Does it glorify God?

3. How can you let God's Word change your attitude towards your current single status?

4. What are some ways that you can let your singleness be about God and furthering the kingdom?

5. What are some advantages to your single status? How can God use you, as a single woman?

18

Calling all the Single Ladies!

SARAH BUBAR

Status: Single

That's what my Facebook says on the info section of my profile. That's right. I. Am. Single. It's true; like a large banner stamped across my homepage, *single*.

February is a dreaded month for most singles when even shopping heightens a single woman's awareness to the fact that she is single. I remember growing up, the goal for the average high school girl was to like someone – *anyone* – for the month of February just so that come Valentine's Day, you would get *something* in the way of a valentine. Now, some 20 years later, February approaches and still brings with it an idea that something is missing from my life.

But is it?

It's been a while now since the Lord has radically done His work in my life in this area and true heart-contentment made its home in my heart, but even still, I find there are twinges of dissatisfaction that awaken in me the idea that I'm still without that "significant other." When those feelings arise, I must go back in time and remember what it was the Lord taught me. There are FIVE MYTHS in regards to singleness that I used to have before the Lord changed my thinking. Five assumptions that I had about marriage and God's will for my life. Five misconceptions that, even in my 30s, I'm still having to replay in my heart. I share them with you in the hope that you will learn sooner than I did.

MYTH #1: I'LL BE HAPPY IF I'M MARRIED BECAUSE I WON'T BE ALONE ANYMORE.

Whoa! What a lie! Reading this statement now, it's hard for me to even believe that I thought this way. But I did. I thought that marriage would be the cure-all for the loneliness blues. I mean, my parents are happy and they're married. Everyone in my church was married; my teachers were married; my youth leaders were married. If someone asked me in college where I saw myself in five years, the first word out of my mouth would be "married." I didn't know what I would be doing, or where I would be, but I was sure that I wouldn't be unmarried in the ambiguous task.

I was 21 when God first started to really abolish this myth I had created in my mind. I say "first started" because like with most lessons that are deep-seated in desire, this has been a process of learning that my sweet Lord has faithfully walked me through. It was after studying the life and story of the Samaritan woman in John 4 that I realized that marriage does not equal happiness. This woman had been married five times already and she wasn't any closer to happiness than she was before. I looked at her and saw a woman who was so empty inside that she was living with a man after being married five times already just to feel like someone out there cared for her. Then she met Jesus, a man who did care for *her*, not just for what she could do for him. I may shake my head in shame for her because she allowed herself to be used in exchange for fleeting feelings and momentary happiness, however, I must swallow my pride and realize we all do this to a certain extent.

Maybe we don't marry the man, but how often have we dated someone or been in a relationship with someone solely based on how it made us feel. I know I've done that before! It's nice knowing that someone out there in the world is thinking about you, thinks you're special. And there is a sense of happiness that comes in this kind of relationship, however short-lived it may be. This was the motivation for the Samaritan woman. This temporary happiness was why she again found herself in another senseless relationship.

TRUTH: WE MUST REALIZE THAT OUR FULFILLMENT AND TRUE HAPPINESS DOES NOT COME THROUGH HUMAN RELATIONSHIPS BUT THROUGH OUR RELATIONSHIP WITH CHRIST.
When that woman came to the well for water that afternoon, she had no idea what was waiting for her, and she certainly had no clue what she'd be walking away with. She came unhappy, alone and rejected, and left fulfilled, truly happy and wanted. That was what Christ was able to offer her at that well; that is what God was trying to teach me. I will never be truly happy with my life, no matter the status, unless I am happy in my relationship with Christ. HE is the source of my joy; HE is the sustainer of my peace; HE is my fulfillment. When we look outside of Christ to find what only Christ can give, we will always be searching for more.

MYTH #2: I'LL FEEL COMPLETE IF I'M MARRIED. I'LL HAVE ACCOMPLISHED SOMETHING WITH MY LIFE.
This statement would fly in the faces of both our Lord Jesus Christ and, according to many scholars, Paul, for neither of these men were married, and yet both fundamentally changed the course of human history.

But those are men, and I'm a woman. Can women accomplish something great in life single? Definitely! My mind immediately goes to biblical examples such as Ruth,

Rahab, Anna, and Miriam. Ruth is an exemplar of the Proverbs 31 woman, and yet the crux of her written story covers the time in her life when she wasn't married. In fact, once she gets married, Scripture stops talking about her except to say that she played a part in the genealogy of Christ. Rahab's story plays out much the same way and each mention of her faith highlights a time in her life when she was unmarried (Josh. 2:6; Heb. 11:31; James 2:25). Anna was a widow for most of her life and all of her ministry, and there is no mention of Miriam *ever* having a husband although she played a *key part* in Israel's exodus and Moses' rise to leadership.

Each of these women is a shining example of singleness coupled with accomplishment. But unless you feel like these *biblical* examples aren't applicable enough, let's consider these "modern day" single women: Amy Carmichael, Lottie Moon, Sophie Muller, Carolyn McCulley, and Nancy Leigh DeMoss. These are just a few single women in history past and present who have done major things for Christ, something their marital status could not thwart. When studying their lives, we see when God calls a woman to do something, He equips her to do His calling.

TRUTH: COMPLETENESS IS ONLY FOUND IN CHRIST!
The first chapter in Ephesians is one of my favorite passages to go to when I need to be reminded of all that I am in Christ and all that I have because of Christ.

- He has blessed me with every spiritual blessing in Christ (v. 3).

- Even before Creation, He chose me to be holy and blameless (v. 4).

- Through His blood, I have redemption and the forgiveness of sin (v. 7).

- He *lavishes* grace on me (v. 8)!!!

And that's just a few of them! Read the whole chapter if you really want to be encouraged! As Christians, we must reconcile with the fact that we have been given everything we need in Christ. As women wanting to live radically for Him, we must realize that this includes our love life. My completeness is ONLY found in Christ, not mostly, only!

MYTH #3: IT MUST BE GOD'S WILL FOR ME TO GET MARRIED AT SOME POINT BECAUSE I WANT IT SO BADLY.
Surely if it wasn't his will, he'd take the desire for marriage away! This myth was so hard for me personally to come to terms with because I believed it whole-heartedly for *years*! I have journals filled with pages and pages of prayers to God asking Him to "take away" my feelings, to "make me not like so-and-so." When I moved to Texas, I found a box of them as I was down-sizing my life for the big move. I sat on the floor of my bedroom in my parents' house laughing at the 16-year-old self, the 18-year-old self, and sadly enough the 24-year-old self. It's like I never learned. I just kept praying and praying, expecting God to take that desire for marriage away. It wasn't until a couple of years ago that the Lord *really* hit me over the head with this:

TRUTH: IN LIGHT OF ETERNITY, IT DOESN'T MATTER ONE BIT IF I ENTER HEAVEN MARRIED OR SINGLE. WHEN I STAND BEFORE THE LORD, THE ONLY THING THAT WILL MATTER IS WHAT I'VE DONE WITH CHRIST!
I still recite this principle to myself on certain days. It is a constant reminder of where my focus should be, on Christ and not myself. When I look to Scripture, I see scores and scores of verses that talk about God's will, and in almost every circumstance (Rom. 12:2; Eph. 6:6; 1 Thess. 4:3, 5:18; 1 Pet. 2:15, 4:2) where it says, "This is the will of God," it's about my *character* not my Facebook status; it never mentions marital status in connection with

the will of God. This leads me to believe that God is more concerned about me becoming WHO I should be than who I should be WITH; in fact, if I focus on BEING who God wants me to be, He will work out the details of my life way better than I could!

MYTH #4: I JUST WANT THIS! AND IF I DON'T GET IT, IT MUST BE A PUNISHMENT OF SOME KIND.

I've lost count the number of times I have misused Psalm 37:4, *Delight yourself in the sight of the Lord, and He shall give you the desires of your heart.* I heard myself confess sins to God in hopes that my singleness wasn't a punishment for them. Like a spoiled child, I have heard my sinful nature question the very love God has for me because He wouldn't give me what I wanted. I have seen the root of jealousy grow within my deceived heart because God was fulfilling the dreams of friends around me while I stood here – single! Like a child throwing a tantrum, I have watched myself clutching on to relationships that God was weeding from my life. I have shouted at God, "You told me to delight. Well, I did, and it STILL didn't get me what I wanted" as if Psalm 37:4 was a magical equation.

So what does it mean if it's not a magic equation for getting what I want? The word delight means "to give great pleasure, satisfaction; please highly." When applying this definition to Psalm 37:4, I see that I am to give great pleasure to God, to find my satisfaction *in* God and in my relationship with Him. How do I do this? By following the principles found in the rest of Psalm 37.

1. Don't worry or be jealous (v. 1).

2. Trust in the Lord (v. 2).

3. Do good (v. 2).

4. Commit your way to the Lord (v. 4).

5. Be still before the Lord and wait patiently for Him (v. 7).

6. Don't get mad (v. 8).

As I begin to do these things in an effort to be satisfied in the Lord, guess what begins to happen? The things that I thought I wanted, I might not want anymore. The ideals that I held so high for my life might not seem all that important anymore. Why? Because of this:

TRUTH: Truly delight yourself in the Lord, and your desires will change – guaranteed!
My desires change to God's desires and what He wants for my life. As Spurgeon says, "Men (in our case, women) who delight in God desire, ask for nothing but what will please God; hence it is safe to give them *carte blanche*. Their will is subdued to God's will, and now they may have what they will."[1]

MYTH #5: If I never get married, then there must be something wrong with me!
I have to tell you, I can actually hear the younger version of myself saying these things in my head as I type them out because I used to truly believe these lies! And ladies, *these are lies!* Straight from Satan himself! To think that there must be something wrong or defective with you is to deny the solid truths of Psalm 139. For *I am fearfully and wonderfully made* (v. 14), God *hems me in – behind and before* (v. 5), God's thoughts of me *outnumber the grains of sand* (vv. 17-18), He *scheduled my days before one of them came to be* (v. 16).

---

1   Charles H. Spurgeon (abr. by David Otis Fuller), *The Treasury of David*, Grand Rapids, MI: Kregel Publications, (1976).

TRUTH: God is sovereign and GOOD ALL THE TIME!

If you're not married, it's because GOD, IN HIS GOOD-NESS, has ordained that you will bring Him more glory *single* than *married*. Jerry Bridges says it well: "God never pursues His glory at the expense of the good of His people, nor does He ever seek our good at the expense of His glory. He has designed His eternal purpose so that His glory and our good are inextricably bound together."[2] It is with this truth that my beliefs must change from what *I think* is good for my life to submitting to what *God knows* is good for my life.

If you are like me, these truths are going to be something that you need to work through, to process. They are truths that you are going to have to be reminded of; some days, you may have to be reminded of them a couple of times. And just when you think you've got it, February will show up on your calendar. Don't be discouraged. I know the process; and I know the peace.

Allow God to lead you through both.

Questions That Make You Go "Hmmm"

1. Which of the five myths do you relate to the most and why?

2. What are some of your own myths about singleness that you believe/have believed?

3. What do you think Scripture says is the truth about them?

4. What are some good things you think God has for your single life?

---

2   Jerry Bridges. *Trusting God: Even When Life Hurts*, Colorago Springs, CO: NavPress (2008).

19

Break Up's Shouldn't Break You

Diane Montgomery and Gabrielle Pickle

Between the two of us, we've had pretty much every bad breakup a girl can have. The one where the girl begs the guy not to leave – yup. The one where he ends things, but continues to call and text to boost his ego, and she lets him – been there. The one where the girl sobs pathetically while asking him what was wrong with her, why wasn't she good enough?... sadly, yes. The one where she can't face the guy who still really likes her, so she ignores him for weeks?... uh huh. The one where she refuses to stop texting him after the break up, hoping he will realize his mistake and ask her back – check. The one where she is so straightforward that he breaks down in tears – ouch, yes.

Oh, the tragic antics of a girl with a broken heart. These antics prolonged our suffering, crushed our confidence and made us wallow in desperation. It took time growing in the Lord, but both of us eventually learned that such break-up antics made the break up hurt so much more. Desperation, disillusionment and distrust are simply not God's plan for his child – even after a break up. As believers, we should be turning to the Lord with our pain, rather than drowning our pain in the old guy, a new guy, a carton of ice cream, or angry chick music.

THE BROKEN-HEARTED

He lied. He lost interest. He found someone else. He didn't love you like you loved him. The reason doesn't really matter, because he ended things and you are heartbroken. As freshly devastated females, our natural reaction usually includes tears, ice cream, self-pity, pajamas, anger, bad hair, bitterness, fast-food, and denial. But as women who claim that Jesus has transformed their lives - doesn't that mean how we handle break-ups has also undergone a transformation? Since we have the power and love of God, shouldn't our recovery from a broken heart reflect Christ? We believe so!

DON'T ASK WHY

Ah, closure. That elusive phantom that follows relationships and drives normal women to bouts of angry questions and incessant sobbing. Lets face it, asking "why?" immediately after a breakup isn't some healthy, meaningful search for character improvement or how you can learn from past experiences. No, it's either pleading with your ex to validate what you had together or it is a desperate attempt to find out what you can change so he will take you back.

Knowing why he's breaking up with you won't actually give you emotional closure, it will only make you obsess more. Knowing is not going to help; it doesn't make the pain any less, and it doesn't help you heal any faster. The guy cannot be your source of validation, because once he's gone or has let you down, then your worth is shattered. No guy should be the source or confirmation of your worth. What we are actually searching for after a breakup is something that only Christ can give us.

When it comes to your broken heart, the only one who can truly give you closure is God. But closure doesn't usually come in the form of answers, it comes from **being with God.** And it's when we are in His presence that things become clearer and we can see bits and pieces of what God is doing in our lives. The Scriptural example of this is Job – a godly, wise and wealthy man in the Old Testament. God allowed Satan to test Job (Job 1–2) to the point that he lost his wealth, his children died, his wife cursed him, and he was afflicted with boils all over his body. Job understands grief and suffering. In the 40+ chapters of Job, he feels anger, despair, insult, abandonment, confusion, and humiliation. It isn't until Job 38-41 that God finally replies. And He doesn't provide the answers to all of Job's questions. Instead, God questions Job, "Are you God, that you question Me?" And in the final chapter, we see Job get closure about everything that has happened to him, not because he got answers, but because he saw God clearly and fell on his knees in worship (Job 42:1-6).

When you focus on what's wrong with you, why weren't you "good enough," or why he doesn't like you enough, **you** are the focus of your break up. And as a girl who has given her life to Christ, shouldn't even the emotional and painful parts of our life glorify Christ? In fact, isn't it in those times of pain and sorrow that we have the greatest opportunity to witness to the world – because we have the power of a risen Lord to get us through an ugly break up?

Don't go to the guy, go to God. Calling him, texting him, crying to him, thinking about him, and wallowing in the pain isn't going to make the problem any better. The only one that can heal your broken heart is the Great Healer, himself. David prays, *[Lord] hear me and answer me. My thoughts trouble me and I am distraught.* (Ps. 55:2), *[h]ear my prayer, O LORD; listen to my cry for mercy.* (Ps. 86:6) *and I pour out my complaint before Him; before Him I tell my trouble* (Ps. 142:2). God alone can provide the comfort, love, validation, and healing you need.

DON'T DO UGLY
When some stupid guy hurts you, the first reaction is to lash out. You want to bad mouth him to all your friends,

trash his treasured car, burn his pictures, pray that his hair falls out, ostracize his new girlfriend, air his dirty laundry on Facebook, let his friends know what a jerk he is.

Those reactions come straight from our hurt girl flesh. Jesus died on the cross to overcome the flesh with the spirit. Through Jesus we have the strength and power to rise above our hurt and anger to live in forgiveness and grace. Now forgiveness doesn't mean excusing sinful behavior, but rather it is allowing God to handle your ex while you move on in freedom. Paul tells the church at Thessalonica, **Be at peace** *among yourselves. And we urge you, brothers, admonish the idle, encourage the fainthearted, help the weak,* **be patient with them all. See that no one repays anyone evil for evil, but always seek to do good to one another and to everyone.** *Rejoice always, pray without ceasing,* **give thanks in all circumstances***; for this is the will of God in Christ Jesus for you* (1 Thess. 5:13-18).

Did you hear that? God calls his children to choose **peace**. Be **patient**. Repay evil behavior with **good behavior**. Give **thanks**. That means no slashing tires or smashing windows. No low blows which you hope will hurt him like he's hurt you. No dating one of his guy friends to make him jealous. No yelling, screaming or crazy girl drama. As a sister in Christ, you are not allowed to have any ugly breakup. If things do turn ugly, it should never be because you got revenge, said nasty things, pitched a fit, or stooped to ugly. You are a daughter of God, an ambassador of Christ on this earth, and acting out in anger only taints the Gospel and damages your witness. As his sister you're still to do him good, no matter how much he hurt you or did you wrong.

Take the high road - believe me, the world will notice! With all the songs and movies about torching his stuff and making the cheater pay, the world expects you to go postal after a breakup. So when you live in grace, wisdom and forgiveness - the world will want to know why. And how amazing would it be if your breakup story was leading someone to Christ because of your post-up witness?

THE HEARTBREAKER

You noticed someone else. You got bored with him. You can't see a future with him. You recognize that he isn't emotionally healthy. Whatever the reason, deciding to end the relationship is often the easy part, it's having to look into his eyes and say those words that makes us want to hurl. Breakups aren't easy for either party, but as believers we have a responsibility to handle breakups well. It is because the guy in question is your brother in Christ and our actions are a witness to the world. Since we have the power and love of God, shouldn't how we break up with a guy reflect Christ? We believe so!

Don't Avoid It

Part of being radically changed by Christ is treating others how you would want them to treat you. It is the 2nd greatest commandment in the Bible, after all! So would you want him to avoid you, rather than being upfront, honest in love, and unselfish about breaking up? Would you want him to stop calling you so you're wondering for weeks what's going on, what's happened, why he suddenly just dropped off the face of the earth? Part of the your new breakup "routine," as a radically changed daughter of God, is treating your brother in Christ with respect and kindness, just like you would want.

Ignoring his calls, ducking behind friends, avoiding him, hoping he will get the message is so not okay. This is your brother in Christ, show him respect. A letter will not do. Neither will an email, or a text, or a voicemail or a tweet. The only thing that works is you being honest with him, even it makes you uncomfortable because you're loving him as Christ loves you. Treat him with honor just as you would want him to treat you with honor.

So whatever you wish that others would do to you, do also to them.

(Matt. 7:12)

Let love be genuine. Abhor what is evil; hold fast to what is good. Love one another with brotherly affection. Outdo one another in showing honor.

(Rom. 12:9-10)

DON'T TRY TO BE HIS FRIEND OR COUNSELOR

As a girl, when we have had to hurt someone, we usually want to make it better. We want to lessen the hurt factor by being a "good friend" to the guy as he tries to recover from this emotional devastation.... Don't. It's cruel. He has to get over you and he can't do that if you are being all sweet and nice and girlfriendy. You are not his girlfriend, you have to let other people in his life be there for him. It's not your place anymore. Yes, you are to love your brother in Christ, but after a breakup loving him means giving him space to heal.

When you talk to him, be honest and clear. This isn't the time to wander around the issue – but be tenderhearted. Many a guy has said that the worst thing a girl can say when initiating a break up is, "You're such a great guy but..." Girls usually try to soften the blow to his heart by giving him compliments, which to him are pretty much useless and just make things worse and confusing. In his mind he's thinking, "If I'm so great then why are you breaking up with me?" "If I'm one of the best guys you've ever dated, then why aren't you continuing to date me?" In trying to be his friend, you're going to end up hurting him more. You've decided that you don't want to be his girlfriend so you have to start acting like an ex-girlfriend, a kind, Christ-like ex-girlfriend that is. Don't try to puff up his ego or counsel him by telling him how many others girls would love to date him. All that does is send him mixed signals.

Pray for him – absolutely. Be kind when you see him – always. Speak well of him to other people – without question. But give him space to heal, as much time and distance as he needs.

> A new commandment I give to you, that you love one another: just as I have loved you, you also are to love one another. By this all people will know that you are my disciples, if you have love for one another.
>
> (John 13:34-35)

> Finally, all of you, have unity of mind, sympathy, brotherly love, a tender heart, and a humble mind.
>
> (1 Pet. 3:8)

TO END HAPPILY EVER AFTER

Whether you ended things with him or he broke up with you, there are truths that apply to every girl who wants to honor God as much in the end as in the beginning of her relationship.

1. GET YOUR CORE TOGETHER

Girlfriends – the kind who love Jesus – can help get you focused on God's truth, help you fight the lies that creep in, and even bring you some brownies and a hug to ease the pain. They are incredibly helpful in intercepting your phone before you start texting your ex and holding you accountable throughout the healing process. Plus, these girls are hands down your best prayer warriors during this time!

Satan is going to use this time to fill your head with lies about your worth/future and he's going to try to tempt you to make unwise choices in your emotionally vulnerable state. Your girlfriends help you during breakups by praying for you and giving you Truth to fight Satan's lies. They are your allies and they can do battle with you.

One of the most wonderful things about being a believer are the people who are there to pray over you and bear with you through life's most hurtful seasons, not to mention they can bring a lot of fun into your life when things don't feel like sunshine and rainbows. So, surround yourself with girls that are going to fill your life with truth and honesty during the healing process. They're God's gift to you!

2. CONSTRUCT HEALTHY BOUNDARIES

After a breakup, we are vulnerable and often find ourselves in a not-so-wise emotionally-driven state. You're feeling insecure, angry, crushed, and depressed – resulting in uninhibited or unwise choices. That's why you need your godly friends' support and accountability. But you also need God's word to guide you in the next steps (Prov. 11:14; 24:6). Scripture gives you the wisdom to set up healthy boundaries which will guard your heart and stop those emotion-driven crazes.

This isn't the time to be his friend either. It's a time to put distance between you both to allow your hearts to heal. It's not mean to not want to be friends; it's a healthy boundary to protect you both. Maybe in the future when both hearts have fully repaired and moved on, then there can be some sort of friendship. But until then it's best to steer clear of each other, as much as possible. You broke up for a reason. Your heart is hurting and it needs time to heal, which takes putting up healthy boundaries. That means emotional, physical and mental space.

3. FIND THE RIGHT DISTRACTIONS AND REBOUNDS

Most girls have a way of getting over a guy and it's usually different depending on the girl. Some choose the "I'm going to hate him till I don't love him" approach because it makes you think you're shutting off your emotions for him so you can't feel the loss and immense hurt of rejection. While others choose the infamous "rebound." How many times have you heard someone say "The best way to get over someone is by getting on with the next one." Rebounds are popular because they get your mind off the guy that broke your heart and get it focused on a newer, cuter guy ... one who hasn't hurt you. But both of these fleshly coping mechanisms don't actually solve the problem, they only mask it for a time.

Neither of these truly solves your problem, nor do they point you to the only one who can heal your heart completely. As women who claim to love God, our rebound should always be God (Ps. 119:50). If you need a distraction, go to God. If you need some companionship, affection, to be loved or desired – God gives you that and so much more! But you know where you get that? From the Bible! It's God's letter to you, showing you who He is, how much He cares about you, and how that changes who you are.

4. BE OPEN TO LEARNING

How many times do we ask ourselves after a breakup, "What was the point of all this, Lord? Why would you guide me to date this guy to get me hurt in the end?" When the breakup is fresh so is the pain and that sometimes clouds whatever reason you may have. But your pain isn't pointless. God has a purpose in everything He does - His glory and your good. There is always a lesson to learn, but you must be humble and teachable.

First, ask the Lord what He wants you to learn from the breakup and relationship. Open your heart to Him and He will be faithful to answer. Time with God will give you perspective and the wisdom to see what was not healthy or right in your relationship. If you let Him, God will help you learn from your past relationships so that your future relationships can be radically different. He can show you what raised the bar for you and what should never happen again. Ended relationships, good or bad, can be something you look back on with thanks because they brought you closer to God, grew you as a woman of God and transformed your future dating experiences.

How you break up matters just as much as who you date or why you date. Use them as times to glorify God, honor your brother in Christ, and show the world that Christ has radically changed every part of your life ... even the most difficult and heartbreaking moments.

QUESTIONS THAT MAKE YOU GO "HMMM"

1. God pays attention to your breakups so what have you been portraying to Him?

2. How do you think your breakup reactions have portrayed to the world?

3. What are things that you can do, other than turning to a new boy, that will enrich your life? New hobbies, sports, ministry opportunities?

4. Write out three things you can learn from past breakups. Then, write three things that your breakups have taught you about God.

Recommended Reading

As you can probably tell the Bible has been the biggest influence in our lives but over the years there have been some other books, which have impacted us greatly. These are some of those books about everything from dating, feminism, modesty, and biblical womanhood. We've read them, we've loved them, and we highly recommend them!

Becoming a Woman Who Pleases God: A Guide to Developing Your Biblical Potential. Lisa Tatlock and Pat Ennis. Moody Publishers. 2003, (336 pgs).

Come Walk With Me: A Woman's Personal Practical Guide to Knowing God and Mentoring Others. Carole Mayhall. Waterbrook Press, 2010, (224 pgs).

Girls Gone Wise: In a World Gone Wild. Mary Kassian, Moody Publishers. 2010, (272 pgs).

The Feminist Mistake. Mary Kassian, Crossway, 2005, (336 pgs).

Lady in Waiting: Becoming God's Best While Waiting for Mr. Right. Jackie Kendall and Debby Jones, Destiny Image Publishers. 2005, (442 pgs).

Let Me Be a Woman. Elisabeth Elliot, Living Publishers, 1999, (192 pgs).

Lies Women Believe: And the Truth that Sets Them Free. Nancy Leigh DeMoss, Moody Publishers, 2008, (288 pgs).

Lies Young Women Believe: And the Truth that Sets Them Free. Nancy Leigh DeMoss and Dannah Gresh, Moody Publishers, 2008, (208 pgs).

The Look: Does God Really Care? Nancy Leigh DeMoss. Revive Our Hearts, 2003, (53 pgs).

Mr. Smith: Revolutionize the Way You Think About Sex, Purity, and Romance. Eric Ludy and Leslie Ludy, Thomas Nelson, 2007. (240 pgs).

Passion and Purity: Learning to Bring Your Love Life Under God's Control. Elisabeth Elliot, Fleming H. Revell, 1984, 2002, (192 pgs).

Radical Womanhood: Feminine Faith in a Feminist Culture. Carolyn McCulley, Moody Publishing, 2008, (224 pgs).

Secret Keeper: The Delicate Power of Modesty. Dannah Gresh, Moody Publishers, 2010, (96 pgs).

When Sinners Say "I Do": Discovering the Power of the Gospel for Marriage. Dave Harvey, Shepherd Press, 2007, (189 pgs).

Bibliography

Austen, Jane. *Pride and Prejudice*. Mineola, NY: (Dover Thrift Editions), Dover Publications, 1995.

Benrendt, Greg and Tuccillo, Liz. *He's Just Not That Into You*. New York, NY: Simon Spotlight Entertainment of Simon & Schuster, Inc., 2006.

Bridges, Jerry. *Trusting God: Even When Life Hurts*. Colorado Springs, CO: NavPress, 2008.

Franck, Dennis. "Single Adults – A Population Group Too Large to Ignore", *Enrichment Journal* [online journal], 2012.

Lee, Ang, dir. *Sense and Sensibility*. Based on novel by Jane Austen. Columbia Pictures, 1995. (DVD-Sony Pictures Home Entertainment, 1999).

Ludy, Eric and Ludy, Leslie. *When God Writes Your Love Story*. Colorado Springs, CO: Multnomah Books, 2004.

Mother Teresa with Devananda, Angelo and Scolozzi, Angelo. *Jesus, The Word to be Spoken: Prayers and Meditations for Every Day of the Year*. Ann Harbor, MI: Servant Publications, 1998.

Ortlund, Jani. *Fearlessly Feminine*. Colorado Springs, CO: Multnomah Books, 2000.

Spurgeon, Charles H. *The Treasury of David*, abr. by David Otis Fuller. Grand Rapids, MI: Kregel Publications, 1976.

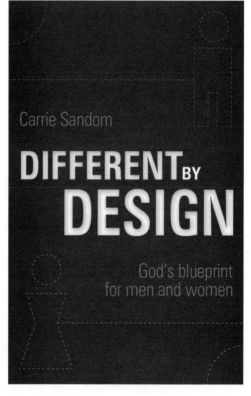

Carrie Sandom

DIFFERENT BY DESIGN

God's blueprint
for men and women

ISBN 978-1-84550-782-4

Different by Design

God's blueprint for men and women

CARRIE SANDOM

Carrie Sandom, along with a rising tide of like-minded Christians, is concerned about the growth of feminism in our society, our families and our churches—and the detriment this poses to all three. She clearly presents the problem and leads readers along the path to restore God's design to its rightful place.

Just as relationships in the Godhead are equal yet diverse, working together in unity and order, so are these characteristics to be reflected in the way men and women relate to one another. Scripturally grounded, *Different by Design* presents a biblical context for the roles of men and women in marriage, the church and the workplace, with present-day implications for each.

She argues convincingly that the differences between men and women go much deeper than the biological and, far from being oppressive, the complementary nature of their relationship is part of God's loving design for human flourishing.

Vaughan Roberts,
Rector of St Ebbe's, Oxford and Director of the Proclamation Trust

Carrie gives practical encouragements to live out our God-given roles, particularly in our families and churches, liberating us to be who God created us to be and inspiring us to do the work he created us to do.

Keri Folmar,
wife of John Folmar, pastor, United Christian Church of Dubai,
United Arab Emirates

With practical insights and scenarios, women especially will find this resource both biblical and culturally relevant.

Margaret Elizabeth Köstenberger,
Adjunctive instructor of Women's Studies at Southeastern Baptist Theological
Seminary, Wake Forest, North Carolina

Carrie Sandom is Associate Minister for Women and Pastoral Care at St John's Church, Tunbridge Wells, UK. She served in women and student ministry for almost 20 years.

THE

ENVY

OF

Eve

FINDING CONTENTMENT IN
A COVETOUS WORLD

MELISSA B. KRUGER

ISBN 978-1-84550-775-6

The Envy of Eve

Finding Contentment in a Covetous World

MELISSA B. KRUGER

The Envy of Eve will help readers to understand how desires grow into covetousness and what happens when this sin takes power in our hearts. Covetousness chokes out the fruit of the spirit in our lives, allowing discontentment to bloom. The key to overcoming is to get to the root of our problem: *unbelief* – a mistrust of God's sovereignty and goodness.

- Illustrated by stories of covetousness from the Bible,

- Tackles key areas like relationships, possessions, circumstances and abilities.

- Thought-provoking Scripture studies

I commend this fine new book … with a prayer that we all read and follow her Biblical counsel to fully understand the condition we are in and flee quickly to the One who truly satisfies our deepest longings and our true desires.

Michael A. Milton,
Chancellor, Reformed Theological Seminary, Charlotte, North Carolina

Through biblical examples and sympathetic counsel we are pointed again and again to the delivering power of the Lord Jesus Christ.

Faith Cook,
Author of *Troubled Journey*, Derbyshire, England

With I've-been-there understanding and been-in-the-Word insight, Melissa Kruger helps us to look beneath the surface of our discontent, exposing our covetous hearts to the healing light of God's Word.

Nancy Guthrie,
Author of the *Seeing Jesus in the Old Testament Bible Study* series,
Nashville, Tennessee

Melissa Kruger serves as Women's Ministry Coordinator at Uptown Church in Charlotte, North Carolina.

Christian Focus Publications

publishes books for all ages

Our mission statement –

STAYING FAITHFUL

In dependence upon God we seek to impact the world through literature faithful to His infallible Word, the Bible. Our aim is to ensure that the Lord Jesus Christ is presented as the only hope to obtain forgiveness of sin, live a useful life and look forward to heaven with Him.

REACHING OUT

Christ's last command requires us to reach out to our world with His gospel. We seek to help fulfil that by publishing books that point people towards Jesus and help them develop a Christ-like maturity. We aim to equip all levels of readers for life, work, ministry and mission.

Books in our adult range are published in three imprints:

Christian Focus contains popular works including biographies, commentaries, basic doctrine and Christian living. Our children's books are also published in this imprint.

Mentor focuses on books written at a level suitable for Bible College and seminary students, pastors, and other serious readers. The imprint includes commentaries, doctrinal studies, examination of current issues and church history.

Christian Heritage contains classic writings from the past.

Christian Focus Publications Ltd,
Geanies House, Fearn, Ross-shire,
IV20 1TW, Scotland, United Kingdom.
www.christianfocus.com